Novak Djokovic

By United Library

https://campsite.bio/unitedlibrary

Table of Contents

Introduction

Djokovic is one of the most dominant tennis players in the world.

This biography tells the story of how he became one of the best and offers an inside look at his Serve to Win technique.

Novak Djokovic is a Serbian professional tennis player who is currently ranked world No. 1 in men's singles tennis by the Association of Tennis Professionals (ATP). He has won 17 Grand Slam singles titles, the fourth most in history, and held the No. 1 spot in the ATP rankings for a total of 294 weeks, which is second only to Roger Federer. His serve-and-volley game and low center of gravity make him one of the best defenders on the tour. He is also known for his mental strength and often comes back from deficits to win matches.

Djokovic has won numerous awards, including the Laureus World Sportsman of the Year, BBC Overseas Sports Personality of the Year, and ESPN's Best Male Tennis Player. In 2020, he was named one of Time magazine's 100 most influential people. Djokovic was born in Belgrade, Yugoslavia (now Serbia) in 1987.

His parents are self-employed entrepreneurs and have a pizza restaurant chain. He began playing tennis at age four and was soon recognized as a prodigy. He turned professional in 2003 and won his first Grand Slam singles title at the 2010 Wimbledon Championships. Since then, he has been one of the most dominant players

You can learn about Djokovic's childhood, his professional career, and what makes him one of the best tennis players in history. Plus, you'll get insights into his Serve to Win technique that will help you improve your own game.

Novak Djokovic

Novak Djokovic, born May 22, 1987 in Belgrade (Yugoslavia, now Serbia), is a Serbian tennis player, professional since 2003.

Considered, along with Roger Federer and Rafael Nadal, to be one of the greatest tennis players of all time, Novak Djokovic has won 87 singles titles on the ATP Tour, including 20 Grand Slams, five Masters and 38 Masters 1000. In 2021, by winning for a second time at the French Open, he becomes the first player of the Open Era and the third male athlete in history, after Roy Emerson and Rod Laver, to hold at least two titles in every Grand Slam lift. In 2018, he won the Cincinnati Masters, becoming the only player in tennis history to win all 9 tournaments in this category in singles. Two years later, he repeated his victory at the Cincinnati Masters - relocated to New York due to the Covid-19 pandemic - and became the first and only player in history to achieve the Golden Masters twice, having won at least twice each of the nine Masters 1000. In 2021, he won the Australian Open for the ninth time, making him the only record holder of titles in this major tournament. He won the bronze medal at the Olympic Games in 2008, the Davis Cup with the Serbian team in 2010 and the first edition of the ATP Cup with Serbia in 2020. Winning every Grand Slam and every Masters 1000 at least twice as well as the Masters, Djokovic has the most complete record of the Open Era. Only the Olympic gold medal is still missing from his record.

He reached the world number one spot for the first time on July 4, 2011, and finished number one seven times after the 2011, 2012, 2014, 2015, 2018, 2020 and 2021 seasons, a historical record. He has, to date, spent 369 weeks at the top of the world rankings, which is the all-time record for the number of weeks spent as world No. 1, which he holds since March 8, 2021, ahead of Roger Federer (310). He also holds the record for the number of ATP points achieved by a player in singles, with 16,950 points on June 6, 2016, the day after he was crowned French Open champion, but also the record for the number of points at the end of the year in 2015, with 16,585 points.

At the end of 2021, at 34 years 7 months and 9 days, he is the oldest player to finish at the top of the ATP rankings at the end of the year. He has been voted the top ATP player seven times and has been elected ITF

World Champion seven times, two records he holds alone.

Novak Djokovic won the Petit Slam in 2011, 2015 and 2021, a record he shares with Roger Federer. He is one of only two players in history, along with Rafael Nadal, to win three Grand Slam titles on three different surfaces (hard court, clay, grass) in the same year, 2021, thus achieving the Petit Slam. His 2015 season is considered one of the best in ATP history along with Rod Laver's in 1969 and Roger Federer's in 2006, totaling eleven titles (three Grand Slams, the Masters, six Masters 1000s, and one ATP 500) and a record of 82 wins to six losses.

In 2016, he won the Australian Open for the sixth time and then won the French Open for the first time in his career. This makes him the only player in the Open Era to win five major titles in a row: 2015 Wimbledon, 2015 US Open, 2015 Masters, 2016 Australian Open, 2016 French Open and the first player to hold all four major tournaments simultaneously since Rod Laver in 1969, achieving the Grand Slam straddling two seasons, which some journalists have called the *Djoko Slam* or *Nole Slam*.

After two years marked by injuries and a plunge in the world rankings, in 2018 he returned to winning Grand Slams at Wimbledon and the US Open, continuing in 2019 with his victories in the Australian Open final in three sets against Rafael Nadal, and his fifth Wimbledon success, beating Roger Federer in the final.

In 2020, by winning the Australian Open, he becomes one of only two players, along with Roger Federer, to have won at least one Grand Slam title on five different surfaces, following the replacement of the Australian *Plexicushion* by the *Greenset*. He is also the first player to have won three Grand Slam tournaments in a row four times: in 2011-2012, in 2015-2016, in 2018-2019 and in 2021. In 2021, with his 9[e] victory at the Australian Open, his 18[e] Grand Slam title, he becomes the record holder of Grand Slam titles won on hard court (12, including nine Australian Open and three US Open). He then won his 2[e] French Open, then, one month later, his 6[e] Wimbledon. He then became the co-record holder of 20 Grand Slam titles with Rafael Nadal and Roger Federer. While he is in the race to achieve the first Grand Slam in a year since Rod Laver in 1969, he is beaten in the final of the US Open by Daniil Medvedev.

In January 2022, he was expelled from Australia after a ten-day political and legal imbroglio following his arrival in the country to play the 2022 Australian Open without being vaccinated against Covid-19. This affair with worldwide repercussions deprives him of a potential tenth victory in Melbourne and a 21[e] record Grand Slam success.

Biography

The son of Serbian skiers Srđan and Dijana Djoković, who were converted to the restaurant business, Novak Djoković began playing tennis at the age of five. His two brothers Marko and Đorđe, born in 1991 and 1994, also have ambitions to become professional tennis players; Marko sometimes plays doubles with him.

Privacy Policy

In addition to his native language, Novak Djokovic is fluent in English and Italian, and during tournaments he may also speak German, French or Spanish.

Novak and Jelena Djokovic have two children: a son Stefan and a daughter Tara.

Career

1993-2004: origin and junior career

When Novak Djokovic's parents moved to Kopaonik, there was no tennis court near their restaurant. However, in the late 1980's, when little Novak Djokovic was just starting to take his first steps, three tennis courts were built across the street from the family restaurant (these courts were destroyed by NATO in 1999 during Operation Allied Force).

Jelena Genčić, who had already discovered Monica Seles and Goran Ivanišević, opens a tennis camp in the summer of 1993. Novak, then six years old, spends his morning watching the exchanges. Jelena noticed him, and asked him to come if he wanted to learn, "in the discipline". The next morning, the little Djokovic joined Jelena, but not only with his racket: he also had a big bag with his stuff folded inside, a bottle of water and a banana, "like a professional. Jelena asks him if his mother has prepared his bag. The child glares at her and answers: "I want to play tennis".

She also tells of seeing a child in Kopaonik who, at the age of six, knew what he wanted, telling her with aplomb that he wanted to play, to win, to win everything.

After three days with Novak, Jelena wants to meet her parents and tells them "you have a golden child". The parents, at first reluctant, are convinced by Jelena's seriousness. Srđan, her father, then decides to sacrifice everything to give Djokovic every chance to succeed. During the 1990s, Serbia was at war and money was far from flowing in the Djokovic household. At the age of 12, Novak Djokovic joined Nikola Pilić's academy in Munich, Germany.

He turned professional in 2003 at the age of 16. In 2004, he was a semi-finalist at the Australian Open as a junior in both singles and doubles with Scoville Jenkins.

2005-2006: debut, first ATP titles

At the beginning of 2005, he was ranked 188^e at 17 years old.

In early 2006, he was ranked 78^e at the age of 18. That year he became known to the general public, especially for his brilliant performance at the French Open, where he eliminated three seeds, reaching the quarterfinals against Rafael Nadal; in this match he had to withdraw due to a back injury after losing the first two sets.

He won two tournaments, in Amersfoort and Metz, and reached the final of the Umag tournament.

He also played a semifinal at the Zagreb Tournament and a quarterfinal at the Rotterdam Tournament, where he was defeated in the final set tiebreaker by eventual tournament winner Radek Štěpánek.

These great performances allowed him to finish 2006 at the 16^e world rank at 19 years old.

2007-2010: the rise to power

2007: Accelerated learning, first Grand Slam final at the US Open, first two Masters 1000 victories

The year 2007 begins for him with a victory at the Adelaide Tournament, where he wins the final against Australian Chris Guccione in three sets. He then went on to reach the round of 16 at the Australian Open, where he lost to Roger Federer (6-2, 7-5, 6-3). After° losing in the first round in Marseille, Djokovic reached the semifinals in Rotterdam and then the quarterfinals of the Dubai Open, where he once again lost to world No. 1 and eventual winner Roger Federer.

He confirmed his good form in March when he reached the final of the Indian Wells Masters, a final he lost 6-2, 7-5 to Spain's Rafael Nadal. It was his first Masters Series final but he repeated the performance the following week in Miami.

This time he won the tournament against Guillermo Cañas (6-3, 6-2, 6-4) without losing a single set of the fortnight and eliminating Rafael Nadal in the quarterfinals, thus obtaining his first victory over the Spaniard. He became the youngest winner of the tournament and one of only 18 players under the age of 20 to enter the *Top 10*. After this victory, he becomes number seven in the world and declares that his goal is to become number one in the world.

His twenty-four wins in three months have moved him to second place in the Race Rankings, just four points behind Roger Federer and fifth in the ATP Technical Rankings.

At the beginning of May, he won in Estoril against the Frenchman Richard Gasquet: (7-6^7 , 0-6, 6-1).

In June, the French Open begins. Djokovic passes the first two rounds without too much difficulty and then wins in five sets one of the most beautiful matches of the fortnight against the surprising French player Olivier Patience (7-6^2 , 2-6, 3-6, 7-6^4 , 6-3). In the round of 16, he quickly eliminated the Spaniard Fernando Verdasco in three sets (6-3, 6-3, 7-6^1). He then defeated Russia's Igor Andreev (6-3, 6-3, 6-3) thanks to some good variations. He is now in the semifinals, the first of his career in Grand Slam, against the great favorite of the event, Rafael Nadal. After two hard-fought sets, the Serbian lost (7-5, 6-4, 6-2) in two and a half hours. At this event, he was awarded the Bud Prize, which is given to the "revelation of the international circuit, the seed of tomorrow's tennis". This performance allowed him to move up from sixth to fourth place in the world.

At Wimbledon, after playing ten *tie-breaks* (eight won) in the previous rounds, including against Lleyton Hewitt (7-6^8 , 7-6^2 , 4-6, 7-6^5) in 4 hours and 13 minutes and Márcos Baghdatís (7-6^4 , 7-6^9 , 6^3 -7, 4-6, 7-5) in 4 hours and 59 minutes, he reached the semifinals, where he met Rafael Nadal again. This time, he managed to win the first set, but gave up in the third set due to injuries, certainly caused by the long matches played in the previous days; the score was (6-3, 1-6, 1-4 ab.).

At the Umag tournament (Croatia, clay court), where Djokovic is seeded No.° 1, he passed the first round easily, against the Spaniard Pablo Andújar (158ᵉ in the ATP rankings), in two sets (6-1, 6-3). But in the second round, he was eliminated by his Serbian compatriot and friend Viktor Troicki, then 176ᵉ world player, in three sets (6-2, 4-6, 5-7). He also participated in the tournament in doubles with his younger brother, Marko Djokovic. The two Serbs did not get past the French pair Mathieu Montcourt-Edouard Roger-Vasselin (5-7, 1-6).

On August 12, he won the Canadian Masters Series after defeating American Andy Roddick, Spain's Rafael Nadal in the semifinals (7-5, 6-3) and world No. 1 Roger Federer of Switzerland in the final ($7-6^2$, 2-6, $7-6^2$). Since Rafael Nadal and Roger Federer are ranked as the top two players in the world, Djokovic is the first to beat them in the same tournament. With this performance, he became the first player since Boris Becker in 1994 to beat three top-five players in the world in a single tournament.

At the Cincinnati tournament (Ohio/USA - Hard), Djokovic loses to Carlos Moyà in the second round (6-4, 6-1).

The US Open begins, and Djokovic advances to the second round at the expense of Robin Haase (replacing Mario Ančić, forfeit), (6-2, 6-1, 6-3). In a much more intense match against Radek Štěpánek, he advances to the round of 16 (6^4 -7, 7-6^5 , 5-7, 7-5, 7-6^2), and then defeats Argentina's Juan Martín del Potro in 3 sets (6-1, 6-3, 6-4) to advance to the round of 16. Djokovic continued his journey, first by reaching the quarterfinals, thanks to a victory over Juan Mónaco (7-5, 7-6^2 , 6^6 -7, 6-1). Then he took his revenge from Cincinnati by eliminating Carlos Moyà (6-4, 7-6^7 , 6-1) to reach the semifinals, where he easily defeated Spain's David Ferrer (6-4, 6-4, 6-3). In the final, he met Roger Federer of Switzerland, ranked 1er in the ATP rankings, against whom he lost (7-6^4 , 7-6^2 , 6-4). This first Grand Slam final earned him a triumphant welcome back to Serbia, with Prime Minister Vojislav Koštunica waiting for him at the airport.

A week after this feat, Djokovic and his Serbian colleagues Janko Tipsarević, Nenad Zimonjić and Viktor Troicki, get Serbia into the Davis Cup World Group. To do so, they beat Australia led by Lleyton Hewitt on the clay court (Indoor) in Belgrade, Serbia. In the first match, Djokovic gets the better of Peter Luczak, then the Australians come back to 1-1 with Hewitt's victory over Tipsarević (6-2, 3-6, 4-6, 6-1, 6-1). With the Zimonjić/Djokovic pair winning against the Hanley/Hewitt pairing, the Serbians take the lead at 2-1. With Lleyton Hewitt out due to an infection, it was Chris Guccione who tried, in vain, to prevent Serbia from entering the world group against Novak, to whom he lost (6-3, 7-6[3] , 7-6[5]).

On October 8, he wins the Vienna tournament, his 5[e] title of the year and 7[e] career, by eliminating the American Robby Ginepri, then the Czech Tomáš Zíb. Djokovic defeated Argentina's Juan Ignacio Chela with difficulty (saving two match points), then defeated Italy's Andreas Seppi in the semis before winning the title over Switzerland's Stanislas Wawrinka in two sets (6-4, 6-0).

In Madrid, Djokovic lost in the semifinals to David Nalbandian with the score of (4-6, 6^4 -7), despite having eliminated Fernando Verdasco, Mario Ančić and Juan Carlos Ferrero.

At the Paris-Bercy Masters, Djokovic lost his first match against Frenchman Fabrice Santoro in two sets (6-3, 6-2), a match in which Djokovic "did not play with the dignity of his rank of n° 3 in the world" and "missed his match", due to, among other things, 34 unforced errors, half of the Frenchman's points. And it's a difficult end to the year for Djokovic, who, poorly recovered from a recent operation, lost his group matches at the Masters in Shanghai to David Ferrer, Richard Gasquet and Rafael Nadal (6-4, 6-4), for a total of 3 defeats out of 3 matches played.

Djokovic finished the year with 68 wins out of 84 matches played and reached the semifinals at Wimbledon, the French Open and the US Open final for the first time in his career. He reached the 3^e world ranking, which is his best ranking. In addition, he is the only one (since Boris Becker in 1994) to beat in the same tournament (at the Montreal Masters) 3 players in the top 5 at the time, namely Roger Federer (1er), Rafael Nadal (2^e) and Andy Roddick (5^e). Djokovic also achieved his highest doubles ranking, reaching 3 .^{e}

2008: The consecration: 1er Australian Open and 1er Masters

Novak Djokovic begins his season with the Hopman Cup, where he and his compatriot Jelena Janković reach the final against the Americans Serena Williams and Mardy Fish. But they lose this final, 2 games to 1 *(Djokovic having won his singles, Jankovic lost his and both having lost the doubles).*

During the Australian Open, Novak Djokovic reassures his fans after a calamitous end of 2007. He successively eliminated Benjamin Becker, Simone Bolelli, Sam Querrey, Lleyton Hewitt, David Ferrer and qualified for the final by beating the world number 1 Roger Federer (7-5, 6-3, 7-6^5), and all this without losing a single set.He became the first player to beat Federer in three sets in a Grand Slam tournament since Gustavo Kuerten at the 2004 French Open, ending the Swiss' streak of 10 consecutive Grand Slam finals. After a spectacular battle, Djokovic finally got the better of the Frenchman with a score of (4-6, 6-4, 6-3, 7-6^2), thus succeeding Roger Federer as the winner of this tournament. He is the first Serbian in the history of tennis to win a Grand Slam singles tournament (men and women combined).

Serbia's first round Davis Cup match was then against defending champion Russia. Following the withdrawal of Djokovic - suffering from fever - for the first singles, and Janko Tipsarević, also ill, Russia quickly takes the lead to 2-0, thanks to the victories of Nikolay

Davydenko at the expense of Viktor Troicki and Mikhail Youzhny against Nenad Zimonjić. The Novak Djokovic/Nenad Zimonjić pair then defeated the Russian pair Mikhail Youzhny/Dmitri Toursounov and Serbia came back to 2-1. Against Nikolay Davydenko in the No. 1 match, Djokovic outdistances the unbeatable Russian and leads two sets to none, before being caught up in the fatigue of illness and accumulated matches, and having to drop out (as a result of the dropout, he had to go to the hospital for a checkup).Serbia is eventually eliminated by Russia with a score of 3-2, after Viktor Troicki defeats Dmitri Toursounov in the optional match.

Djokovic then entered the Open 13, against the advice of his entourage. Out of shape, he was eliminated in the quarter-finals by French titleholder Gilles Simon in three sets (2-6, 7-6[6] , 3-6).

He then cancelled his participation in the Rotterdam tournament, in order to better prepare for the Dubai Open and then defend the points of his final in Indian Wells and those of his victory in Miami last year.

At the Dubai Open, Novak Djokovic lost in the semifinals to the American Andy Roddick, number 6 in the world, and future winner of the tournament, in two sets (7-6[5] , 6-3).

The following week, he travels to Indian Wells to play in the first Masters Series of the season. He played a perfect tournament, beating Andreas Seppi, Philipp

Kohlschreiber, Guillermo Cañas, Stanislas Wawrinka and Rafael Nadal without losing a set. °In the final, he faced the American Mardy Fish, who had defeated Nikolay Davydenko, Lleyton Hewitt, David Nalbandian and world No. 1 Roger Federer. After a match with many twists and turns, the Serbian won (6-2, 5-7, 6-3).

He followed this up with a real setback when he lost in the second round of the Miami Masters, where he was the defending champion, beaten by South African Kevin Anderson in three sets (6^1 -7, 6-3, 4-6). This setback is very detrimental to his desire to become the world's No. 1 player because he loses the benefit of the points he earned the previous season at this same tournament. However, Djokovic remains confident: he is far ahead of his first direct pursuer in the rankings, the Russian Nikolay Davydenko, and will have the opportunity to catch Nadal during the clay court season, during which the Spaniard will have more than 2,000 points to defend.

He reached the semifinals of the Monte Carlo Masters before bowing out to Roger Federer when he was down 6-3, 3-2 on aggregate. In front of journalists, he explained that he had a sore throat.

Two weeks later, on May 11, 2008, he won the Rome Masters against the astonishing Swiss Stanislas Wawrinka, after a hard-fought final (4-6, 6-3, 6-3). He successively defeated Belgian Steve Darcis, Russian Igor Andreev, Spaniard Nicolás Almagro in the quarterfinals and Federer's loser, Czech Radek

Štěpánek, in the semifinals. This is the fourth Masters Series of his young career.

At the Hamburg Masters, he made it all the way to the semifinals, where he faced Rafael Nadal. This match will remain in the annals of clay court matches. Indeed, the players played at an extraordinary level simultaneously. Djokovic leads 3-0 in the first set with his unplayable tennis, then Nadal, who has not been seen for a long time, comes back into the match and both players play at the highest level for three sets. Nadal won (7-5, 2-6, 6-2), and the next day he won the tournament over Roger Federer.

Roland Garros 2008: Novak Djokovic successively defeated Germany's Denis Gremelmayr (4-6, 6-3, 7-5, 6-2), then Spain's López Jaen (6-1, 6-1, 6-3) before defeating the American Wayne Odesnik (7-5, 6-4, 6-2) and then France's Paul-Henri Mathieu (6-4, 6-3, 6-4). In the quarter-finals, he met the young Latvian prodigy Ernests Gulbis. The latter posed a problem for him thanks to his formidable serve, frequently exceeding 210 km/h. Nervous, the Serb managed to defeat him in three sets. In the semifinals, he faced Rafael Nadal, who had beaten his compatriot Nicolás Almagro (6-1, 6-1, 6-1), and lost in three sets (6-4, 6-2, 7-6[3]) after the Spaniard was only shaken in the third set. He missed the opportunity to take Nadal's second place in the ATP rankings.

The following week, he participated in the Queen's Club tournament. In the quarter-finals, he defeated Lleyton

Hewitt in two straight sets (6-2, 6-2), and gave world number 8 David Nalbandian no chance in the semi-finals (6-1, 6-0) in just 45 minutes. He was beaten in the final by Rafael Nadal in a superb match, lost 7-6[6], 7-5, 2 sets during which he had managed to get a break lead each time.

At Wimbledon, he eliminates Michael Berrer in the 1[er] round (7-5, 2-6, 6-3, 6-0) but loses in the 2[e] round against Marat Safin in 3 sets (6-4, 7-6[3], 6-2), it is the first time in 5 Grand Slam tournaments that Novak Djokovic does not reach the semi-finals.

At the Canadian Masters, where he is the title holder, he is eliminated in the quarter-finals by Andy Murray in two sets (6-3, 7-6[3]).

At the° Cincinnati Masters, Novak Djokovic won a sumptuous semifinal against Rafael Nadal, already assured of becoming the world's No. 1 player and thought to be invincible (6-1, 7-5). He ended the Spaniard's 32-match winning streak and advanced to the final. In the final, however, he lost in two sets to Andy Murray (7-6[4], 7-6[5]) in 2 hours and 23 minutes of play. At the end of the tournament, Djokovic regained his position as No.° 2 in the ATP Race 2008 rankings (ranking of the best players of the year), behind Rafael Nadal but ahead of Roger Federer.

Novak Djokovic lost in the semifinals of the Olympic Games to Rafael Nadal (6-4, 1-6, 6-4) after a match lasting more than two hours. He left the court visibly touched by this defeat, but will nevertheless win the bronze medal the next day during the match for the 3[e] place which opposes him to James Blake.

Following Novak Djokovic's good performances in Cincinnati and at the Olympics, and Roger Federer's relatively poor performances at these two tournaments, the point gap between these two players is now only 825 points at the end of the Olympics. °The Serb has the opportunity to take away the Swiss' position as world No. 2 if he wins the US Open or if he reaches the final and Federer fails before the quarter-finals.

At the US Open, he reached the semifinals after eliminating Arnaud Clément (6-3, 6-3, 6-4), Robert Kendrick (7-6[6] , 6-4, 6-4), Marin Čilić (6[7] -7, 7-5, 6-4, 7-6[0]), Tommy Robredo (4-6, 6-2, 6-3, 5-7, 6-3) and Andy Roddick (6-2, 6-3, 3-6, 7-6[5]). However, he did not repeat his performance of the previous year, when he was defeated by Roger Federer (6-3, 5-7, 7-5, 6-2) at the final. Thus°, he did not seize the opportunity to steal the world's No. 2 ranking from the Swiss.

Two weeks later, the Serbian entered the tournament in Bangkok, Thailand. He defeated Simon Stadler (6-1, 6-3), then had to battle through the next round to defeat Sweden's Robin Söderling (6-4, 7-5), before defeating Czech Tomáš Berdych in the semifinals (7-5, 6-1). In the final, he met up with Jo-Wilfried Tsonga, whom he had beaten in the Australian Open final, and this time got the better of the world number three (7-6[4] , 6-4).

He loses at the Madrid Masters to Ivo Karlović, the best server on the circuit with Roddick, in 2 tie-breaks. He participates in the Paris-Bercy Masters, which is the last tournament of the season (apart from the Masters). He has never shone there and wants to end his season on a high note. Indeed, the year before, he was knocked out by Santoro in the first round. This year, he made it through the first round without a hitch against Dmitri Toursounov after dropping the second set (6-4, 4-3). In the round of 16, he met up with Jo-Wilfried Tsonga for their third meeting of the year with a win all around. He was taken out in three sets by the Frenchman (6-4, 1-6, 6-3) playing below his best level. Tsonga will be the future winner of the event.

At the Masters Cup, Novak Djokovic found himself in the gold group with Jo-Wilfried Tsonga, Nikolay Davydenko and Juan Martin del Potro. He won his first match against del Potro (7-5, 6-3). Thanks to Tsonga's defeat of del Potro and his victory over Davydenko (7-6^3, 0-6, 7-5), he qualified for the semifinals before even playing his third group match against Tsonga, which he lost 1-6, 7-5, 6-1. In the semifinals, he faced Frenchman Gilles Simon, who he had lost to in Marseille. This time, he beat him in three sets (4-6, 6-3, 7-5) and qualified for the final. He won the final against Davydenko (6-1, 7-5) and won his first Masters Cup.

At just 21 years old, Novak Djokovic has had the best season of his career, with a Grand Slam title (Australian Open), two Masters Series titles (Indian Wells and Rome), and the Masters Cup title. He remains No.° 3 in

the world, but is only 10 points away from Roger
Federer's No.º 2 ranking.

2009 : Disappointments in Grand Slam, victory in Paris-Bercy and 4 other finals in Masters 1000

Novak Djokovic began his season at the Brisbane Open where, seeded No.° 1, he lost in the first round to Ernests Gulbis (6-4, 6-4). Benefiting from a wildcard at the Sydney tournament, he needed to reach the final to take away Roger Federer's place as world No.° 2, but after easily eliminating Paul-Henri Mathieu and Mario Ančić, he failed in the semifinals against Jarkko Nieminen.

The Serbian then tries to retain his title at the Australian Open. In the 1er round, he defeats the qualified Andrea Stoppini before beating the Frenchman Jérémy Chardy in the 2^{d} round and Amer Delić in the 3e round more difficultly. In the 1/8 finals, he defeated Márcos Baghdatís in 4 tight sets (6-1, 7-6^1 , 6^5 -7, 6-2). He gives up in the quarterfinals against Andy Roddick, being down 2 sets to one and tired after his match against Márcos Baghdatís.

After a week of rest, he participated in the Dubai Open, where he won the 1er title of his season his semifinal against Gilles Simon (3-6, 7-5, 7-5 in 2 hours 46). The following weekend, Djokovic was selected to play in the Davis Cup match between Serbia and Spain. He lost the first singles match to David Ferrer of Dubai (6-3, 6-3, 7-6^4). He then participated in the Indian Wells tournament, where he was the defending champion, but reproduced the same scenario as at the Australian

Open a month earlier, Andy Roddick eliminated him in the quarterfinals.

The° Serbian had a difficult start to the season, but the following week at the Miami Masters, he bounced back by eliminating Jo-Wilfried Tsonga in the quarter-finals and then world No. 2 Roger Federer in the semi-finals. However, he lost to Andy Murray in the final.

Despite two defeats in the Davis Cup on clay a few weeks earlier, Novak Djokovic started the clay court season rather well. At the Monte-Carlo Masters, he became convincing again by beating Fernando Verdasco (6-2, 4-6, 6-3) and reached the final for the first time in his career. In the final, he met up with Rafael Nadal and managed to take a set from the Majorcan, who had not conceded a set since 2006. However, the Serb was physically overwhelmed at the end and finally broke (3-6, 6-2, 1-6).

Djokovic° followed up with the Masters in Rome, where he reached the final by eliminating the world's No. 2 Roger Federer in the semifinals, as he did in Miami. But he lost for the eighth time in a row on clay to Rafael Nadal ($7\text{-}6^2$, 6-2). The following week, he won his second tournament of the season at home in Belgrade on clay against Poland's Łukasz Kubot with a score of 6-3, $7\text{-}6^0$. He leaves the 3^e world ranking in the ATP rankings on May 11, overtaken by Andy Murray, a position he then occupied since July 2007.

He° has the opportunity to regain his 3^e world ranking if he reaches the final of the 2009 Madrid Masters, for which he stumbled in the semifinals against the world's No. 1 Rafael Nadal (3-6, 7-6^5 , 7-6^9) of a record duration of 4 hours and 2 minutes, where he obtained 3 match points in the tie-break of the 3^e set. °At the French Open, he lost in the 3rd round to Philipp Kohlschreiber of Germany; the Serb had made two consecutive semi-finals in Paris. He admits later that the match in Madrid against Nadal weighed heavily on his mind until Wimbledon.

On grass, the following week, at the Halle Open in Germany, he lost in the final against another German Tommy Haas, then 41^e in the ATP, with the score of (6-3, 6^4 -7, 6-1). It was against this same German player that Novak Djokovic lost at the Wimbledon tournament, at the stage of the quarterfinals (7-5, 7-6^6 , 4-6, 6-3).

His North American tour began with a quarter-final at the Canadian Masters. After a first round match against Peter Polansky, he raised his game to beat Mikhail Youzhny. But he failed in the quarter-finals against Andy Roddick in two tight sets. Nevertheless, in Cincinnati, he picked up the pace. He successively eliminated Ivan Ljubičić, Jeremy Chardy, Gilles Simon and Rafael Nadal without losing a set.In the final, he was powerless against Roger Federer, untouchable from the first to the last point (6-1, 7-5). He said at the time of the presentation of the trophies: "Of the whole match, it is now that I will have been closest to the title".At the US Open, he was again defeated by the

Swiss (7-6^3 , 7-5, 7-5) for the second year in a row in the semifinals, after successively eliminating Ivan Ljubičić, Carsten Ball, Jesse Witten, Radek Štěpánek and Fernando Verdasco.

He does not resume his season until the tournament in Beijing in early October. He makes his comeback, successive winners of Victor Hănescu (6-3, 7-5), Viktor Troicki (6-3, 6-0), Fernando Verdasco (6-3, 1-6, 6-1), Robin Söderling (6-3, 6-3) and one of the revelations of this end of season, Marin Čilić (6-2, 7-6^4).He follows with the Shanghai Masters 1000. Withdrawals of Roger Federer and Andy Murray, Rafael Nadal's lack of fitness and the premature defeat of Juan Martin del Potro put him as the great favorite of the tournament, but in the semifinals, after three solid victories though, he was eliminated in the finish by a huge Nikolay Davydenko (6-4, 4-6, 6^1 -7), who the next day crushed Rafael Nadal for the title.

Far from being discouraged, Novak Djokovic is determined to salvage his 2009 season, which has been far less brilliant than 2008, and so he is lining up in Basel, the home of a certain Roger Federer, after two quick victories over Andreas Beck (6-3, 7-5) and Jan Hernych (6-0, 6-0), before struggling against Stanislas Wawrinka. He came within two points of being eliminated, but managed to pull through (3-6, 7-6^5 , 6-2). The hardest part is yet to come: in the semifinals, he faces Radek Štěpánek who is almost untouchable at the net, saves three match points and reverses the course of the match to win in three sets (6^4 -7, 7-5, 6-2).

After a two-day break, Novak Djokovic played the first round of the Paris-Bercy Masters 1000 against Juan Mónaco (6-3, 7-5). He won in the first round against Arnaud Clément (6-2, 6-2), before emerging victorious in the quarterfinals against French Open finalist Robin Söderling (6-4, 1-6, 6-3). In the semifinals, he met Rafael Nadal (6-2, 6-3). In the final, the Serbian meets Gaël Monfils. He got the flu at 6-2, 3-0. He loses the second set and after a third set, finds himself in a tiebreak. He wins with a final score of 6-2, 5-7, 7-6^3 .

After a week of respite, he was back at the London Masters. His first match saw him win in almost 3 hours against the Russian Nikolay Davydenko (3-6, 6-4, 7-5). He thus takes his revenge for the Shanghai Masters 1000. But Djokovic is tired: in the next match, after a tight first set, he collapses against Sweden's Robin Söderling (7-6^5 , 6-1). For his last group match, Djokovic faced Rafael Nadal. The first set is a contest of unforced errors between the tired Serb and the Spaniard not at his best. Novak Djokovic finally won the first set in a tiebreak, before raising his level in the second set, winning in just over two hours (7-6^5 , 6-3). But Nikolay Davydenko's victory in the evening against Robin Söderling eliminated the Serb. At the end of the 2009 season, Novak Djokovic has played no less than ten finals, winning five. This is the record of the season, as well as his personal record.

2010: Ups and downs, second final at the US Open

Novak Djokovic begins his season with the Kooyong exhibition tournament in Melbourne, where he is beaten by Fernando Verdasco, future winner, in the semi-finals (6-1, 6-2).

At the Australian Open, he advanced to the quarterfinals without much trouble, losing only one set in four matches, to Marco Chiudinelli in the second round. After eliminating tournament surprise Łukasz Kubot in the round of 16, he faced his great rival Jo-Wilfried Tsonga in the quarters, in an epic rematch of the 2008 final of the same tournament between them. After an indecisive match lasting nearly four hours, the Serbian lost for the fifth time in seven matches to the Frenchman (6-7[8] , 7-6[5] , 1-6, 6-3, 6-1), but after the match, he mentioned gastric problems that would have handicapped him. Nevertheless°, the early defeat of Rafael Nadal in the quarters combined with that of Andy Murray in the final allows Novak Djokovic to become, February 1er 2010, No. 2 in the world ATP rankings for the first time in his career, behind Roger Federer who leads him by more than 3000 points.

In Rotterdam, he lost in the semi-finals to Mikhail Youzhny. He kept his title in Dubai by taking his revenge in the final against the same Russian.

His American tour is very disappointing. He loses in Indian Wells in 1/8 against Ivan Ljubičić. He does even worse in Miami, where he is eliminated from the start against Olivier Rochus.

The season on clay of the Serb is less good than last year, Djokovic lost in Monte Carlo and Rome respectively in 1/2 and 1/4, both times against Fernando Verdasco. He puts his title on the line again in Belgrade where he gives up in 1/4 after having lost to Filip Krajinović.

At Roland Garros, he started the tournament without much of a track record. The first few rounds are followed by victories without too much difficulty. He finally lost in the quarter-finals to Austrian Jürgen Melzer after leading two sets to nothing.

He followed up with the Queen's tournament but was beaten by Xavier Malisse in three sets and started his grass court season in the worst possible way.

At Wimbledon, after a scare in the first round against Olivier Rochus and an unconvincing five-set victory, he fell short of the final, defeated in three sets by Czech Tomáš Berdych. However, his presence in the last four, coupled with the premature defeat of Roger Federer, allowed him to take away from the Swiss his place as n° 2 in the world, Rafael Nadal occupying the place of n° 1.

His preparation for the US Open resulted in a defeat in Toronto in 1/2 against Roger Federer and then an elimination in 1/4 in Cincinnati against Andy Roddick.

At the US Open, Djokovic had a very good tournament despite a difficult first round against Viktor Troicki during which he lost two sets. After defeating Philipp Petzschner, James Blake, Mardy Fish and Gaël Monfils, he met Roger Federer in the second half of the tournament. In a sublime five-set match, in which the Serbian saved two match points, Djokovic won after almost four hours of play (5-7, 6-1, 5-7, 6-2, 7-5). He only failed in the final against the world's n° 1 Rafael Nadal in four sets (6-4, 5-7, 6-4, 6-2).

He then resumed his season in Beijing, a tournament where he is the defending champion. In the continuity of his good tournament in New York, he disposes of David Ferrer in the final in two sets. He won his second trophy of the season. In addition, he was very consistent throughout the tournament.

At the Shanghai Masters 1000, Novak Djokovic made a very solid start to the tournament. However, in the semifinals, he came up against the bone of Roger Federer and could only lose (7-5, 6-4). °The Swiss then took his revenge from the US Open and took the Serbian's place as the world's No. 2 player and kept it until the end of the year.

He played in the Basel tournament where he reached the final against the same opponent as last year, Roger Federer. While Djokovic won the previous year, the Swiss won in three sets (6-4, 3-6, 6-1).

At the Paris-Bercy Masters, he comes hoping to retain his title. However, he lost to Michaël Llodra prematurely in the 1/8 finals.

His last tournament before the Davis Cup is one of his most important goals, the Masters Cup. He came out of the group stage in second place after wins over Tomáš Berdych and Andy Roddick despite a hiccup in his second match against Rafael Nadal. He was stopped in the semifinals by the eventual winner Roger Federer in two sets (6-1, 6-4).

On December 3, Novak Djokovic defeated Gilles Simon (6-3, 6-1, 7-5) in the Davis Cup final to tie the match with France (1-1). On December 5, he again provided the tie-breaker for Serbia by beating Gaël Monfils (6-2, 6-2, 6-4) (2-2). On the same day, Serbia won the Davis Cup for the first time in its history.

2011 - 2015: An undisputed champion

2011: Petit Slam, Australian Open, Wimbledon and US Open winner, 5 Masters 1000 winners, World No. 1 and Sportsman of the Year

Novak Djokovic begins his 2011 season at the Hopman Cup exhibition tournament. In his first match, he defeated Andrey Golubev despite a slow start (4-6, 6-3, 6-1). His second match was against Lleyton Hewitt and he was convincing (6-2, 6-4). Against Ruben Bemelmans, he won without any difficulty (6-3, 6-2).

Djokovic starts the Australian Open as well as possible, with an easy win against Marcel Granollers (6-1, 6-3, 6-1). Then he followed up with a more difficult victory over the surprising Ivan Dodig (7-5, 6^8 -7, 6-0, 6-2). He then reached the third round where he defeated Viktor Troicki (6-2, ab). He validates his ticket to the quarters, following a match won with style against Nicolás Almagro (6-3, 6-4, 6-0). He reached the last four of the tournament after a well-played match against Tomáš Berdych (6-1, 7-6^5 , 6-1). °In the semifinals, he faced world No. 2 Roger Federer, who was the favorite after Rafael Nadal's elimination, and beat him in three sets (7-6^3 , 7-5, 6-4). He° wins the Australian Open against world No. 5 Andy Murray (6-4, 6-2, 6-3). The Serbian wins his second Grand Slam tournament at the age of 23, after his first triumph, already in Melbourne, in 2008.

He withdrew from the Rotterdam tournament due to a slight shoulder pain; he had been a semi-finalist in this tournament the previous year.

He made a winning return to the Dubai Open where he retained his title despite a difficult draw. He defeated Michaël Llodra (6-3, 6-3), Feliciano López (6-3, 2-6, 6-4), Florian Mayer (7-5, 6-1) and Tomáš Berdych (6^5 -7, 6-2, 4-2, ab.). He then easily beat Roger Federer in the final (6-3, 6-3), confirming his great form. He defeated the Swiss for the second time in a row without losing a set, just like at the Australian Open.

Djokovic then participated in the Masters of Indian Wells where he defeated Andrey Golubev (6-0, 6-4), Ernests Gulbis (6-0, 6-1), Viktor Troicki (6-0, 6-1) and Richard Gasquet (6-2, 6-4) without losing a set. °He reached the semifinals, where he defeated Roger Federer for the third time in a row (6-3, 3-6, 6-2), taking the No. 2 ranking in the world from him. In the° final, he defeated Rafael Nadal, the world's No. 1 player, after three sets (4-6, 6-3, 6-2). He beats Nadal for the first time in a final (after five defeats).

The Miami Masters follows Indian Wells, with a faster surface and slightly less favorable to the game of Serbia. Novak Djokovic° nevertheless qualified for the round of 16 by easily beating Denis Istomin (6-0, 6-1) and then the American James Blake, former world number 4 (6-2, 6-0). He then reached the final by defeating his compatriot Viktor Troicki (6-3, 6-2), Kevin Anderson (6-4, 6-2) and Mardy Fish (6-3, 6-1). He won his seventh *Masters 1000 title* by defeating Rafael Nadal in the final (4-6, 6-3, 7-6[4]), ending the first part of the season on hard court with a series of 24 wins in as many matches in 2011.

Following a knee pain, and in order to be in shape for the clay court season, he gave up participating in the Monte-Carlo Masters and took a few days off.

He makes his comeback at the Belgrade Open at home. He wins his fifth tournament of the year by defeating Adrian Ungur (6-2, 6-3), Blaž Kavčič (6-3, 6-2), Janko Tipsarević (forfeit) and Feliciano López (7-6[4] , 6-2).

At the Madrid Masters, he reached the quarter-finals without too much trouble, after wins over Kevin Anderson (6-3, 6-4) and Guillermo García-López (6-1, 6-2). In the quarter-finals, he faced and beat the world's No.° 6 David Ferrer (6-4, 4-6, 6-3), one of the strongest men of the clay court season. He qualifies for his 6[e] consecutive final by eliminating the surprise of the tournament, the Brazilian Thomaz Bellucci (4-6, 6-4, 6-1). In the final, he defeated Rafael Nadal in two sets (7-5, 6-4), his first win on clay against the Spaniard. This is his first win on clay against the Spaniard and his 32[e] consecutive wins since the beginning of the season and remains undefeated in 2011.

At the Rome Masters, he continued his superb streak by successively eliminating Łukasz Kubot (6-0, 6-3), Stanislas Wawrinka (6-4, 6-1), Robin Söderling (6-3, 6-

0) and finally Andy Murray (6-1, 3-6, 7-6^2) at the end of a hotly contested match that would be voted at the end of the year as the most beautiful match on the ATP circuit in 2011. In the final, he once again defeated Rafael Nadal (6-4, 6-4) to win his seventh consecutive title, with 37 wins without a single loss. He then set a record for the earliest guaranteed qualification for the year-end Masters Series in London.

In the second Grand Slam of the season, at the French Open, he defeats in the first two rounds the Dutch Thiemo de Bakker (6-2, 6-1, 6-3), as well as Victor Hănescu (6-4, 6-1, 2-3, ab) to qualify for the third round. In the next round, after a match played over two days due to the arrival of the night, he defeats Argentina's Juan Martín del Potro (6-3, 3-6, 6-3, 6-2). He then defeated France's Richard Gasquet (6-4, 6-4, 6-2) in the round of 16, earning his 41^e consecutive victory. He advanced directly to the semifinals thanks to the withdrawal of Italian Fabio Fognini, thus depriving him of a potential 42^e consecutive victory and thus the equalization of John McEnroe's record. Because of this withdrawal, Djokovic did not play for 5 days. He^o resumed the competition on June 3 where his invincibility was stopped in the semifinals by the world's No. 3 Roger Federer. The Swiss won (7-6^5 , 6-3, 3-6, 7-6^5) and prevented the Serb from equaling McEnroe's record. This defeat of the Serbian, combined with the victory of Rafael Nadal in the final against the Swiss, will also allow the Spaniard to remain n° 1 in the world at the end of the tournament, Djokovic being distanced by only 45 points.

During his press conference following his semi-final loss to the Swiss, Novak Djokovic announced his withdrawal from the Queen's tournament which began the following week.

He arrives at Wimbledon, along with Rafael Nadal and Roger Federer, as the tournament favorite. He reached the quarterfinals without difficulty, dropping only one set in four matches against Jeremy Chardy (6-4, 6-1, 6-1), Kevin Anderson (6-3, 6-4, 6-2), Márcos Baghdatís (6-4, 4-6, 6-3, 6-4) and Michaël Llodra (6-3, 6-3, 6-3). In the quarter-finals, he beat the young sensation of the tournament, Bernard Tomic (6-2, 3-6, 6-3, 7-5), then earned a place in the final by defeating Jo-Wilfried Tsonga after a very close match (7-6^4 , 6-2, 6^9 -7, 6-3). On this occasion, he became the twenty-fifth n^o in the history of tennis and reached his first final on the London lawn. In the final, he faced Rafael Nadal for the fifth time this year, and won in four sets (6-4, 6-1, 1-6, 6-3), thus winning his first Wimbledon title, his third Grand Slam. He declared after the match that this first victory at Wimbledon is "the best day of his life".

When the new ATP rankings were released on July 4, 2011, Djokovic had a margin of just over 2,000 points over Rafael Nadal. A monumental reception is held in Belgrade to celebrate his victory and his 1re world ranking, as well as a celebration with more than 100,000 people, before he returns to the courts to prepare for the Davis Cup quarterfinal against Sweden starting July 8. Serbia won 4-1, with Djokovic and

Nenad Zimonjić losing in doubles. In the semifinals, Djokovic and his compatriots will face Argentina.

He played his first tournament as n° 1 at the Montreal Masters 1000, where he was awarded the crystal trophy, being the 25e player in history leading the world tennis. He meets again Jo-Wilfried Tsonga in the semifinals, after dispatching the matches against Nikolay Davydenko (7-5, 6-1), Marin Čilić (7-5, 6-2) and Gaël Monfils (6-2, 6-1). At this level, he benefits from the forfeiture of the Frenchman due to elbow pain, when he was leading clearly(6-4, 3-0 ab.). He wins his 9e title of the season by beating the American Mardy Fish in the final in three sets (6-2, 3-6, 6-4). In doing so, he became the first player to win five Masters 1000 titles in the same year since their inception in 1990, but also the first player since Pete Sampras in 1993 to win a title in his debut as an ATP Tour leader.

At the Cincinnati Masters, he started with two easy wins over Ryan Harrison (6-2, 6-3) and Radek Štěpánek (6-3, 6-3), before advancing to the semifinals after a more difficult victory over Gaël Monfils (3-6, 6-4, 6-3). Once again, he reached the final after Tomáš Berdych withdrew after winning the first set (7-5, ab.). He met Andy Murray again, and for the second time this year, lost the match after withdrawing due to shoulder problems (6-4, 3-0 ab.). Djokovic did not reach the tenth title of the season in this tournament.

At the US Open, he reached the third round after a win over Conor Niland (6-1, 5-0 ab.), then after a controlled match against Argentine Carlos Berlocq (6-0, 6-0, 6-2). He reached the 1/8 finals after his victory against Nikolay Davydenko in three sets (6-3, 6-4, 6-2). In the process, he signed his 60^e victory of the season, for only 2 defeats. In the 1/8 finals, he had more difficulty beating the talented but inconstant Ukrainian Alexandr Dolgopolov, whom he met for the first time ($7\text{-}6^{14}$, 6-4, 6-2). Things get even more complicated in the quarterfinals, where against his compatriot Janko Tipsarević he loses his first set of the tournament, before seeing his opponent give up due to thigh pain ($7\text{-}6^2$, $6^3\text{-}7$, 6-0, 3-0 ab.). In the semifinals, as in 2010, he came close to losing to Roger Federer. With two match points against him in the fifth set, Djokovic found the necessary resources to reverse the trend and finally win the match in a tight and beautiful match ($6^7\text{-}7$, 4-6, 6-3, 6-2, 7-5). For the third time in his career, and for the second year in a row, Novak Djokovic reaches the final of the US Open where he meets Rafael Nadal again. After more than 4 hours of play, Novak Djokovic won in four sets, 6-2, 6-4, $6^3\text{-}7$, 6-1, and won his sixth final in 2011 against the Spaniard. This is the first time he has beaten Roger Federer and Rafael Nadal in a row in the same Grand Slam tournament, becoming one of only two players, along with Juan Martin del Potro, to beat them in the same Grand Slam tournament. The latter had beaten them in his victory at the 2009 US Open. He reinforces his position as the world's n° and continues his exceptional year. With $10.6 million in earnings in 2011, he breaks the record for earnings in a single season in the history of tennis, previously held by

Rafael Nadal. He then withdrew from two tournaments: the Chinese Open and the Shanghai Masters. He returned to the tour at the Basel Open but lost in the semifinals to the 32^e world player, Kei Nishikori in three sets (2-6, 7-6, 6-0). It was his fourth defeat of the season. Unable to play in the Bercy tournament due to a sore shoulder, he still played in the tournament but withdrew after two wins, shortly before the quarter-final match against Jo-Wilfried Tsonga.

At the Masters, he was joined by Andy Murray [3], David Ferrer [5] and Tomáš Berdych [7] in Pool A. He won his first match against the Czech (3-6, 6-3, 7-6^3) but then lost in two sets to the Spaniard (3-6, 1-6). In his final match against Janko Tipsarević [9], Murray's replacement, a win would not guarantee him a place in the semifinals. His compatriot, already eliminated from the race to the semifinals, reduces his chances of qualification by inflicting a sixth defeat this season on the world number one (6-3, 3-6, 3-6.). Berdych's victory over Ferrer seals Djokovic's fate, ending the 2011 season with three Grand Slam titles and five Masters 1000 titles, for a win-loss record of 70-6.

2012: Winner of the Australian Open, finalist at the French Open and the US Open. Second consecutive year at the top of the world tennis rankings

World No. 1 Novak Djokovic is entering a crucial season with two main goals. In addition to the Grand Slam tournaments, the gold medal at the London Olympics, as well as defending his position as leader in the ATP rankings, which is coveted by Roger Federer, are of great interest to him. °In preparation for the Australian Open, he began his season with the Abu Dhabi exhibition, which he won by defeating world No. 5 David Ferrer (6-2, 6-1) in the final.

In the first Grand Slam of the season, the Australian Open, he defeated Paolo Lorenzi (6-2, 6-0, 6-0), Santiago Giraldo (6-3, 6-2, 6-1), Nicolas Mahut (6-0, 6-1, 6-1) and Lleyton Hewitt (6-1, 6-3, 4-6, 6-3) in the first rounds to reach the quarterfinals, where he faced David Ferrer for the second time this season. Despite pain in his left thigh, he won the match (6-4, 7-6^4 , 6-1) and advanced to the semifinals where he eliminated Britain's Andy Murray, ranked fourth in the world, after a very close match (6-3, 3-6, 6^4 -7, 6-1, 7-5 in 4 hours 50 minutes). In the final, he defeated Rafael Nadal for the seventh consecutive time in a memorable final, the longest in the history of the Grand Slam, with a score of 5-7, 6-4, 6-2, 6^5 -7, 7-5 in 5 hours and 53 minutes· .

Then three-time title holder at the Dubai Open, he lost in the semifinals to Andy Murray in two sets (2-6, 5-7). At the Indian Wells Masters, he successively defeated

Andrey Golubev (6-3, 6-2), Kevin Anderson (6-2, 6-3), Pablo Andújar (6-0, 6^5 -7, 6-2) and Nicolás Almagro (6-3, 6-4) before losing to the American John Isner (6^7 -7, 6-3, 6^5 -7)

He won the 30[e] ATP title of his career at the Miami Masters, beating successively Márcos Baghdatís (6-4, 6-4), Viktor Troicki (6-4, 6-3), Richard Gasquet (7-5, 6-3), David Ferrer (6-2, $7-6^1$), Juan Mónaco (6-0, $7-6^5$) and Andy Murray (6-1, $7-6^4$).

In the first round of the Monte Carlo Masters, he defeated Andreas Seppi (6-1, 6-4). On April 19, while he was scheduled to play Alexandr Dolgopolov in the second round in the afternoon, he learned in the morning, while on a training court, that his grandfather had died. Very touched morally, he finally decides not to withdraw from the tournament and beats Dolgopolov (2-6, 6-1, 6-4) in pain. In the next round, he beat Robin Haase (6-4, 6-2). He then defeated Tomáš Berdych (4-6, 6-3, 6-2) to advance to the final where he faced seven-time tournament winner Rafael Nadal. He lost 6-3, 6-1 and ended a seven-match winning streak against the Spaniard.

At the Madrid tournament, he beat Daniel Gimeno-Traver in turn (6-2, 2-6, 6-3) and then Stanislas Wawrinka ($7-6^5$, 6-4) before losing in the quarterfinals to his compatriot Janko Tipsarević (6^2 -7, 3-6).

He then went on to the Rome Masters where he defeated Australian Bernard Tomic (6-3, 6-3) followed by Argentine Juan Mónaco (4-6, 6-2, 6-3). In the quarter-finals, he met up with Frenchman Jo-Wilfried Tsonga, whom he beat (7-5, 6-1). In the semifinals, he faced and defeated Roger Federer (6-2, 7-6[4]) before losing again in the final to Rafael Nadal in two sets (5-7, 3-6).

To finish this season on clay comes the second Grand Slam of the season, Roland Garros. He goes through the first three rounds without too much trouble, successively beating the Italian Potito Starace (7-6[3] , 6-3, 6-1), the Slovak Blaž Kavčič (6-0, 6-4, 6-4) and the French Nicolas Devilder (6-1, 6-2, 6-2). He encountered his first difficulties in the round of 16 against Italy's Andreas Seppi, who won the first two sets before Djokovic rallied to win the next three (4-6, 6[5] -7, 6-3, 7-5, 6-3). As in Rome, he met up with Frenchman Jo-Wilfried Tsonga in the quarter-finals, who gave him a good 4:09 of opposition, winning no less than four match points in the fourth set on the Serb's serve each time, match points that he saved by showing great strength and playing his best tennis, then he dispatched the fifth set (6-1, 5-7, 5-7, 7-6[6] , 6-1). As in 2011, he will meet Roger Federer of Switzerland in the semi-finals. But unlike last year, he beat the Swiss in three sets (6-4, 7-5, 6-3) and met up with Spain's Rafael Nadal for a high-stakes final: if he wins, he will achieve his "Djoko Slam" while Nadal, with a 7[e] French Open title, would dethrone Björn Borg's record. The final, tense between the two men, took place under a growing drizzle, causing many unusual technical errors of the players, and two interruptions of the match. Nadal won the first two sets, but his game was clearly eroding as the rain became even more intense. The Serb adapted better to the situation, and went on an eight-game winning streak in the third set and the beginning of the fourth. Nadal, frustrated by the weather conditions, threw a waterlogged ball at the referee and asked for the match to be postponed. His request was finally granted, and the match was over the next day (which had not happened since 1973 at the French Open). The fourth set is close, but finally won by a more aggressive Nadal, on a double fault on his opponent's serve (6-4, 6-3, 2-6, 7-5). Therefore, the Grand Slam will not be achieved by Djokovic in 2012, so he will not accomplish the Grand Slam by eventually winning the Olympics, which would have been unprecedented. In addition, he takes the opportunity to regain the lead over Rafael Nadal in the ATP rankings, having not reached the last Sunday in Paris in 2011.

On June 6, 2012, he was appointed to be the flag bearer of Serbia at the London Olympics.

He starts his season on grass at Wimbledon, where this year this Grand Slam can also be considered as a preparation tournament before the London Olympics. He passed the first three rounds without much difficulty, eliminating successively Juan Carlos Ferrero (6-3, 6-3, 6-1), Ryan Harrison (6-4, 6-4, 6-4) and Radek Štěpánek (4-6, 6-2, 6-2, 6-2), before qualifying for the quarterfinals by defeating his compatriot Viktor Troicki (6-3, 6-1, 6-3). In the quarter-finals, he defeated Germany's Florian Mayer (6-4, 6-1, 6-4) and lost in four sets to world number three Roger Federer (6-3, 3-6, 6-4, 6-3). The Swiss managed to win the tournament, Novak Djokovic loses the world number one spot to the latter after 53 weeks.

At the London Olympics, he finished at the foot of the podium. He then won the Canadian Masters by eliminating successively Bernard Tomic (6-2, 6-3), Sam Querrey (6-4, 6-4), Tommy Haas (6-3, 3-6, 6-3), Janko Tipsarević (6-4, 6-1) and in the final Richard Gasquet (6-3, 6-2). He participated the following week in the Cincinnati Masters, where he lost in the final to Roger Federer with a score of 6-0, 7-6[7] . This is the first time he has lost a set to Roger Federer by a score of 6-0.

At the US Open, he reached the final by eliminating successively Paolo Lorenzi (6-1, 6-0, 6-1), Rogerio Dutra Silva (6-2, 6-1, 6-2), Julien Benneteau (6-3, 6-2, 6-2), Stanislas Wawrinka (6-4, 6-1, 3-1, ab.), world number eight Juan Martin del Potro (6-2, 7-6[3] , 6-4) and world number five David Ferrer (2-6, 6-1, 6-4, 6-2). However, he lost the final to world number four Andy Murray (6[10] -7, 5-7, 6-2, 6-3, 2-6), after a very competitive match, and therefore did not win his sixth Grand Slam title.

He participated in the 2012 China Open in early October, which he won after beating throughout the tournament Michael Berrer (6-1, 6[3] -7, 6-2), Carlos Berlocq (6-1, 6-3), Jürgen Melzer (6-1, 6-2), Florian Mayer (6-1, 6-4) and finally Jo-Wilfried Tsonga (7-6[4] , 6-2). He then participated in the Shanghai Masters, where he reached the final after eliminating Grigor Dimitrov (6-3, 6-2), Feliciano Lopez (6-3, 6-3), Tommy Haas (6-3, 6-3), and world number seven Tomáš Berdych (6-3, 6-4). He won his thirteenth Masters 1000 in the final against Andy Murray, whom he defeated 5-7, 7-6[11] , 6-3, after winning the tie-break in the second set 13-11 and saving five match points.

On° October 28, world No. 1 Roger Federer withdrew from the Paris-Bercy Masters, where he was the defending champion. As a result, Novak Djokovic is guaranteed to regain the world number one ranking. In addition, also uncertain because of family concerns, the Serbian finally participates in the Paris tournament by making a remarkable entry with a Darth Vader mask for the day of Halloween but loses from his entry into the competition against Sam Querrey (6-0, 6[5] -7, 4-6), after having largely led the American in this meeting (6-0, 2-0). On November 5, 2012, the Serbian regains his throne, amply deserved, at the expense of the Swiss and at the same time takes a fairly large lead after providing a steady work throughout the season.

In the London Masters, he reached the semifinals after beating his three opponents in the group matches: Jo-Wilfried Tsonga (7-6[4] , 6-3), Andy Murray (4-6, 6-3, 7-5) and Tomáš Berdych (6-2, 7-6[6]). Despite being down a set and a break in the second set, he went on to defeat Juan Martin del Potro (4-6, 6-3, 6-2). In the final of the 2012 London Masters, he defeated Roger Federer (7-6[6] , 7-5) after being broken at the beginning of each set, thus winning his second Masters in a high-level match.

He is the first player since Roger Federer (2004-2007) to finish the year n° consecutively.

2013: 4^e Australian Open including the 3^e consecutive, finalist at Wimbledon and US Open, but lost 1re place

World number 1, Novak Djokovic begins his season, as the previous year, with the exhibition tournament in Abu Dhabi, a tournament he won for the second year in a row by easily eliminating David Ferrer in the semifinals (6-0, 6-3) and more difficult Nicolás Almagro in the final (6^4 -7, 6-3, 6-4).

He then represented his country at the Hopman Cup mixed competition with Ana Ivanović as his partner, where they lost in the final to the Spanish pair of Fernando Verdasco and Anabel Medina Garrigues, before heading to the first major tournament of the season, the Australian Open. He started his tournament with ease by eliminating Paul-Henri Mathieu (6-2, 6-4, 7-5) and then Ryan Harrison (6-1, 6-2, 6-3). In the third round, he defeated Czech Radek Štěpánek (6-4, 6-3, 7-5). He advances to the quarterfinals after beating Swiss Stanislas Wawrinka, seeded No.^{o} 15 (1-6, 7-5, 6-4, 6^5 -7, 12-10), where he was trailing 1-6, 2-5 after a splendid match lasting 5 h 2 min. He reached his eleventh consecutive Grand Slam semifinal after defeating Tomáš Berdych (6-1, 4-6, 6-1, 6-4). He advanced to the final after giving world No. 4 David Ferrer a real lesson (6-2, 6-2, 6-1), winning an impressive 85 points to Ferrer's 41 and losing only seven points on his serve. He won the final against Andy Murray in four sets: 6^2 -7, 7-6^3 , 6-3, 6-2, and thus became the first player of the

Open era to win the Australian Open three times in a row.

He then participated in the Dubai Open, where he defeated his compatriot Viktor Troicki in the first round (6-1, 6-4) and Roberto Bautista-Agut in the second round (6-1, 7-6^4). He finally defeated Andreas Seppi (6-0, 6-3) and then in the semifinals Juan Martin del Potro (6-3, 7-6^4) to reach the final. He won the title by beating Tomáš Berdych (7-5, 6-3)[.] . This victory makes him undefeated for 18 matches in official competition, since his defeat in the 2^e round of Bercy against Querrey. This is^e his 3rd consecutive title, after the Masters at the end of 2012, the Australian Open in early 2013 and Dubai.

He then begins his tour on American hard court, with the Indian Wells Masters. To begin with, he beat the Italian Fabio Fognini with difficulty (6-0, 5-7, 6-2) despite a good start, then Grigor Dimitrov (7-6^4 , 6-1). In the next round, he defeated the last man to have officially beaten him, Sam Querrey (6-0, 7-6^6), to earn a spot in the quarter-finals where he faced Jo-Wilfried Tsonga. He easily beat Tsonga, 6-3, 6-1. He was then eliminated in the semifinals, to everyone's surprise, by Juan Martin del Potro, 4-6, 6-4, 6-4, thus suffering his first defeat of the season. He then went on to the Miami Masters, where he defeated Lukáš Rosol (6-1, 6-0) and Somdev Devvarman (6-2, 6-4) in his first rounds, but then lost to Tommy Haas (2-6, 4-6).

Then begins the clay court tour. Djokovic is not sure about the Monte Carlo Masters because of a right ankle injury sustained during the Davis Cup, but he does participate in the event. He was exempted from the first round and played Mikhail Youzhny at the 2^e Tour, beating him in three sets (4-6, 6-1, 6-4). In the next round, he defeated Juan Mónaco (4-6, 6-2, 6-2). He then met Jarkko Nieminen in the quarter-finals, beating him relatively easily (6-4, 6-3) and then defeated Italian Fabio Fognini (6-2, 6-1), who had defeated Tomáš Berdych and Richard Gasquet, to reach the final of the first clay court Masters 1000 of the season. He achieved the feat in the final, beating eight-time defending champion Rafael Nadal (6-2, 7-6[1]). This ended Nadal's 46 consecutive wins in Monte Carlo· . And he becomes the player who has beaten Rafael Nadal the most times on clay since 2005. After 12 days without touching his tennis racket, he appears at the Madrid Masters, where he loses to a young Bulgarian Grigor Dimitrov (6[6] -7, 7-6[8] , 3-6). In the Rome Masters he defeated Albert Montañés (6-2, 6-3) in the second round and Alexandr Dolgopolov (6-1, 6-4) in the round of 16 before losing to Tomáš Berdych (6-2, 5-7, 4-6) in the quarters.

At the French Open, he started his tournament in a decent way by eliminating the young Belgian David Goffin (7-6[5] , 6-4, 7-5), then in the next round Guido Pella (6-2, 6-0, 6-2). In the next round, he got his revenge on Grigor Dimitrov, beating him this time very easily (6-2, 6-2, 6-3). In his next round against Philipp Kohlschreiber, he lost the first set of his tournament, but still qualified for the quarterfinals (4-6, 6-3, 6-4, 6-4). After this match, he pays a vibrant tribute to his former coach Jelena Genčić, who passed away two days earlier in Belgrade at the age of 77, and indicates that he will do everything to win this edition of Roland Garros in her honor.He enters his quarterfinal match against Tommy Haas, the 35-year-old doyen of these French Open tennis events. He won the match in three sets, 6-3, 7-6^5 , 7-5, but he was not without being pushed around.this semi-final so expected since the draw, opposing the seven-time champion Rafael Nadal, will take place. However, he lost the match after an incredibly disputed match with many twists and turns with a score of 4-6, 6-3, 1-6, 7-6^3 , 7-9.

His grass court season continued directly with Wimbledon, where he qualified for the third round without any problems by eliminating Florian Mayer (6-3, 7-5, 6-4) and Bobby Reynolds (7-6^2 , 6-3, 6-1). He then easily defeated Jérémy Chardy (6-3, 6-2, 6-2) after a near-perfect match that included thirty-eight winners and only three unforced errors. In addition, he lost only six points on his serve. He reached his 17e consecutive Grand Slam quarter-finals by defeating Tommy Haas (6-1, 6-4, 7-6^4). In the next round, he defeats Tomáš Berdych (7-6^5 , 6-4, 6-3) to reach the semifinals of a Grand Slam tournament once again. He describes this semifinal, played against Argentina's Juan Martin del Potro, as "the greatest match he has played at Wimbledon. He fought for four hours and forty-four minutes before winning 7-5, 4-6, 7-6^2 , 6^6 -7, 6-3, having had two match points during the second tie-break before del Potro won' . In the final, he was beaten by Andy Murray in a surprising match in which he produced a much inferior tennis than usual, missing most of his smashes, making about forty mistakes and serving poorly. He lost 6-4, 7-5, 6-4 in just over three hours.

He then entered the Canadian Masters Series, where he advanced to the semifinals after defeating Florian Mayer (6-2, 6-1), Denis Istomin (2-6, 6-4, 6-4) and Richard Gasquet (6-1, 6-2). However, he did not participate in the final, following his defeat by Rafael Nadal (4-6, 6-3, 6^2 -7). The following week, at the Cincinnati Masters, the only *Masters 1000* missing from his record, after beating Juan Mónaco (7-5, 6-2) and David Goffin (6-2, 6-0), he lost to John Isner (6^5 -7, 6-3, 5-7).

He then begins the US Open, where he will try to regain the confidence he has lost lately following his slightly disappointing results. In his opening match, he defeats Ričardas Berankis (6-1, 6-2, 6-2), and then in the second round Benjamin Becker (7-6^2 , 6-2, 6-2), although he had to save two first set points. In the next match, he defeated João Sousa (6-0, 6-2, 6-2) and then the Spaniard Marcel Granollers (6-3, 6-0, 6-0) in the round of 16 in just over an hour and a half. He then advanced to the semifinals by defeating Mikhail Youzhny of Russia (6-3, 6-2, 3-6, 6-0). He advanced to his fourth consecutive final at the US Grand Slam, defeating Switzerland's Stanislas Wawrinka in a tight match (2-6, 7-6^4 , 3-6, 6-3, 6-4). He lost for the second consecutive time in a Grand Slam final to Rafael Nadal.

He then competed in the China Open, a tournament that generally works well for him as he is still undefeated after winning in 2009, 2010 and 2012. He began by easily defeating Lukáš Rosol (6-0, 6-3), before dropping a set to Fernando Verdasco (7-5, 2-6, 6-2). He then defeated American Sam Querrey (6-1, 6-2) and Frenchman Richard Gasquet (6-4, 6-2), who defeated David Ferrer. Finally, for the second time this season, he defeated his greatest enemy, Rafael Nadal, in the final (6-3, 6-4), controlling his match well. However, after the tournament, the Spaniard regained the number one ranking in the world from the Serbian based on his best record over the last 12 months. The following week, at the Shanghai Masters, he successively defeated Marcel Granollers (6-2, 6-0), Fabio Fognini (6-3, 6-3), Gaël Monfils (6^4 -7, 6-2, 6-4) in a disputed match, then Jo-Wilfried Tsonga (6-2, 7-5). He won the tournament for the second year in a row, defeating Juan Martin del Potro in the final (6-1, 3-6, 7-6^3), making it a record 20 consecutive wins in China.

He then entered the Paris-Bercy Masters where he had very few points to defend following his poor performance the previous year. In his first match, he beat the young Frenchman Pierre-Hugues Herbert (7-6^3 , 6-3), then John Isner (6^5 -7, 6-1, 6-2), dropping a set. Then, he easily defeated Stanislas Wawrinka (6-1, 6-4), as well as Roger Federer (4-6, 6-3, 6-2) with more difficulties to offer himself a place in the final. He wins the sixteenth *Masters 1000* of his career by beating Spain's David Ferrer (7-5, 7-5)

The following week at the Masters in London with full confidence. In the group matches, he defeated his three opponents, Roger Federer (6-4, 6^2 -7, 6-2), Juan Martin del Potro (6-3, 3-6, 6-3) and Richard Gasquet (7-6^5 , 4-6, 6-3), each time in three sets. He then defeated Stanislas Wawrinka of Switzerland (6-3, 6-3). In a match between the two best players in the world, he won the third Masters title of his career the next day, after a highly controlled match against Rafael Nadal (6-3, 6-4)' . His end of the season was almost perfect because, even though he ended it at 2^e in the ATP rankings, he won the last four tournaments in which he participated and totaled 24 consecutive wins. He added two wins to this streak a few days later in the Davis Cup final, where he defeated Radek Štěpánek (7-5, 6-1, 6-4) and Tomáš Berdych (6-4, 7-6^5 , 6-2). Despite these two victories, his season with the Serbian Davis Cup team did not end ideally, as being the only pillar of his team, Tipsarević and Troicki were absent from the final, they lost 2-3 against the Czech Republic. His main focus regarding the 2014 season will be mostly centered on Grand Slam tournaments.

2014: 2^e Wimbledon, 4^e Masters, finalist at Roland Garros and 1re world ranking

As in 2012 and 2013, Novak Djokovic began his season with the Abu Dhabi exhibition tournament, which he won for the third consecutive time by defeating David Ferrer in the final (7-5, 6-2) after eliminating Jo-Wilfried Tsonga in the semifinals. His official season begins with the Australian Open, where he easily reaches the quarterfinals. °For his 19^e consecutive Grand Slam quarterfinals, he plays the Swiss and seeded No. 8 Stanislas Wawrinka for a rematch of the exceptional match played in 2013, in the round of 16. He loses this anthology match on the score of 6-2, 4-6, 2-6, 6-3, 7-9 after four hours, on a missed volley, and thus ends his series of 28 consecutive victories since his defeat in the final of the US Open 2013 and three Australian Open in a row.

He then participated in the Dubai tournament, where he was the defending champion and four-time winner, and made it through the first two rounds. He qualified for the semi-finals thanks to the withdrawal of Russian Mikhail Youzhny, where he fell to Roger Federer (6-3, 3-6, 2-6), the eventual winner of the tournament.

He then participated in the first *Masters 1000* of the season in Indian Wells. After a quiet first round, he gets rid of the Colombian Alejandro González with difficulty (6-1, 3-6, 6-1). He then defeats one of the men in form at the beginning of the season, the Croatian Marin Čilić (1-6, 6-2, 6-3), then successively eliminates Julien

Benneteau and John Isner to qualify for the final. He wins the first title of his season (the 17^e *Masters 1000*) by taking revenge on Roger Federer (3-6, 6-3, 7-6^3). The following week he was seeded No.^{o} 2 in Miami, Florida. First, he defeated Jeremy Chardy (6-4, 6-3), before benefiting from the withdrawal of German Florian Mayer. He then defeated Tommy Robredo (6-3, 7-5), as well as Andy Murray (7-5, 6-3) after a well-controlled match, and thus earned a place in the last four. He goes directly to the final after a second forfeit in his favor in the tournament, that of the Japanese Kei Nishikori that he had to meet in the semi-finals. In the final, the Serbian easily defeated Rafael Nadal in an incredible and highly controlled match, in 1 hour and 23 minutes with a score of 6-3, 6-3. He thus achieves, for the second time in his career, the Indian Wells-Miami double.

His clay court season then began in mid-April with his home Masters in Monte Carlo, where he was the defending champion. He defeated Albert Montañés (6-1, 6-0) in the first round, and then two days later gave Pablo Carreño Busta a lesson (6-0, 6-1). He then lost a set in a difficult match against Guillermo García-López (4-6, 6-3, 6-1), before losing in the semifinals to Roger Federer of Switzerland (5-7, 2-6), due in part to his wrist, which became very sore during that match. This same pain forced him to withdraw from the Madrid Masters. However, he was able to participate in Rome the following week. In his first match, he defeated Radek Štěpánek (6-3, 7-5) and then Philipp Kohlschreiber (4-6, 6-2, 6-1). He then eliminated

Spain's David Ferrer in a tight three-set match (7-5, 4-6, 6-3), before beating Canada's Milos Raonic (6^5 -7, 7-6^4, 6-3) in the semifinals in another tightly contested duel. In the final, he defeated his direct enemy Rafael Nadal (4-6, 6-3, 6-3) to win his fourth consecutive title. He became the player with the most clay court victories against the Spaniard, adding a 19th *Masters 1000* title to his record.

During the French Open, Djokovic passes Portuguese João Sousa (6-1, 6-2, 6-4) and then Frenchman Jérémy Chardy (6-1, 6-4, 6-2) without problems. In the third round, he drops a set to Marin Čilić (6-2, 6-3, 6^2 -7, 6-4). He then dispatches Jo-Wilfried Tsonga in the round of 16 (6-1, 6-4, 6-1). In the quarters, he faced Canadian Milos Raonic (n° 8) and qualified after a solid match (7-5, 7-6^5, 6-4). For a place in the final, he defeated Latvia's Ernests Gulbis, who had a surprising run, in four sets (6-3, 6-3, 3-6, 6-3). For the second time in the final of the Porte d'Auteuil tournament, he is once again facing Rafael Nadal (n° 1), who has already beaten him five times at Roland Garros. After taking the first set (3-6), Djokovic lost a second set (7-5). Nadal then took advantage of the Serbian's lack of action and his exceptional play to win the third set (6-2), and after several twists and turns, finally broke to win a fifth straight final in Paris, his ninth in all, at the end of a very high-level match (3-6, 7-5, 6-2, 6-4) in 3:31.

Novak enters the Wimbledon tournament as the No. 1 seed° , thanks to the special ranking of the London tournament. He started his championship in a very convincing way by crushing Kazakh Andrey Golubev (6-0, 6-1, 6-4) in the first round. He then won a more competitive match against Czech veteran Radek Štěpánek (6-4, 6-3, 6^5 -7, 7-6^5) in over three hours. He then advanced to the quarterfinals by eliminating Frenchmen Gilles Simon (6-4, 6-2, 6-4) and Jo-Wilfried Tsonga (6-3, 6-4, 7-6^5). There he met the Croatian Marin Čilić for another very close match, however won with a score of 6-1, 3-6, 6^4 -7, 6-2, 6-2 in almost three hours. He once again advanced to the final by eliminating the young Grigor Dimitrov (6-4, 3-6, 7-6^2 , 7-6^7) who fell to Andy Murray in the previous round. For only the second time in their careers, Novak Djokovic and Roger Federer are in the Grand Slam final. This time it was the Serb who prevailed and won the London tournament by beating the Swiss (6^7 -7, 6-4, 7-6^4 , 5-7, 6-4), at the end of a match with many twists and turns lasting nearly four hours. In addition to ending this series of three lost Grand Slam finals (Wimbledon 2013, US Open 2013, French Open 2014), Novak becomes once again world number one in place of Rafael Nadal, a ranking lost at the end of 2013. This second victory in London continues to anchor his name a little more in the legend of tennis, bringing his number of Grand Slam victories to seven, matching Mats Wilander and John McEnroe .

After getting married during the month of July, Novak begins the North American tour with the Toronto Masters 1000, a tournament where he is a three-time winner. The Serbian, who did not make it to the first round, began with a complicated match against

Frenchman Gaël Monfils, which he won 6-2, 6^4 -7, $7\text{-}6^2$ in two hours and forty minutes. In the round of 16, Djokovic faced Jo-Wilfried Tsonga for the twentieth time in their careers. After a mediocre match on his part, he is eliminated against the Frenchman rather dryly with the score of 6-2, 6-2. He goes straight to the Masters 1000 in Cincinnati. In the second round, he had to fight against Gilles Simon but ended up winning 6-3, 4-6, 6-4. However, as in Toronto, Djokovic was eliminated in the third round, this time against Tommy Robredo ($7\text{-}6^6$, 7-5).

Despite his surprising setbacks in the previous two Masters 1000 tournaments, Novak enters the final Grand Slam of the calendar, the US Open, as a heavy favorite with Roger Federer. If some people had doubts about the Serb's motivation (especially regarding his statements that tennis was no longer his priority), his first four matches dispel all doubts. He began by crushing Argentina's Diego Schwartzman (6-1, 6-2, 6-4) in the first round and then easily defeated France's Paul-Henri Mathieu (6-1, 6-3, 6-0) in the next round. American Sam Querrey offered a little more opposition, but still passed the steamroller "Novak" who won this match 6-3, 6-2, 6-2. The Serb then faces German Philipp Kohlschreiber (seeded No.° 22), who defeated John Isner in the 1/16 finals. Novak responded to this first real test and won 6-1, 7-5, 6-4. In the quarter-finals, he faces for the 21e time the Scot Andy Murray. After two titanic sets, Andy injured his back and was no longer able to play at the same level as before. Novak won $7\text{-}6^1$, 6^1 -7, 6-2, 6-4 and qualified for his eighth consecutive semi-final at Flushing Meadows. However, the Serb was eliminated by Japan's Kei Nishikori 6-4, 1-6, 7-6[4] , 6-3. This was the fourth year in a row that he reached the final in New York. It should be noted that never before had Novak lost in a Grand Slam against a younger opponent. In fact, the vast majority of his losses were to Federer, Nadal or Murray (older than a week).

After the disappointment of the US Open, Novak begins the Chinese tour, a series of tournaments where he has always had excellent results. The Chinese Open is no exception to the rule and sees the Serb triumph for the fifth consecutive time. He[o] defeated Spain's Guillermo García-López (6-2, 6-1), young Canadian Vasek Pospisil (6-3, 7-5), top seed Grigor Dimitrov (6-2, 6-4) and Andy Murray (6-3, 6-4). After this excellent tournament, he participated in the penultimate Masters 1000 of the season in Shanghai. After this excellent tournament, he participated in the penultimate Masters 1000 in Shanghai. He started the tournament by eliminating the young Dominic Thiem in the second round (6-3, 6-4). Mikhail Kukushkin of Kazakhstan suffered a similar fate in the third round, losing 6-3, 4-6, 6-4, but still managed to take a set from the Serbian. The Spaniard David Ferrer did not do better and Novak eliminated him 6-4, 6-2 in the quarterfinals. Novak Djokovic meets Roger Federer in the semifinals, the 36[e] time the two players meet. Despite an excellent match, Novak is eliminated 6-4, 6-4 in one hour and thirty-six minutes. It is worth noting that Novak's last defeat in China was in the semifinals of the 2010 Shanghai tournament, where he was also beaten by Roger Federer.

While the Serbian's position as world number one is being challenged by Roger Federer's excellent season, Novak enters the Paris-Bercy Masters, the last Masters 1000 of the season. He will face German Philipp Kohlschreiber in the second round for the third time this season. Like the two previous times, Novak eliminated him easily (6-3, 6-4). He then defeated Frenchman Gaël Monfils (6-3, 7-6^2) for the tenth consecutive time. In the quarter-finals, he perfectly controls the British Andy Murray (7-5, 6-2). He then took his revenge on the Japanese Kei Nishikori who had beaten him at the US Open a few weeks earlier (6-2, 6-3). In the final, he defeated Milos Raonic (6-2, 6-3), thus equaling the record of three victories in Paris-Bercy held jointly with Marat Safin and his coach Boris Becker, and thus winning his twentieth *Masters 1000*, as well as the 600[e] victory of his career .

Of course, he participates during the month of November in the "Masters tournament", the London Masters. He fully succeeds in his entry into the competition on November 10 by easily getting rid of the winner of the US Open, Marin Čilić (6-1, 6-1); then in the second clash, he dryly beats Stanislas Wawrinka including a second set of exception (6-3, 6-0). Finally, he defeats Tomáš Berdych (6-2, 6-2) to finish the group matches, a victory that ensures him to finish the season at the number one spot in the world, for the third time in his career after 2011 and 2012; moreover, it is his 30[e] consecutive indoor victory, his last defeat going back to 2012 against Sam Querrey in Paris-Bercy . He qualified for another *Masters* final by beating Japan's Kei Nishikori (6-1, 3-6, 6-0), a final he won after forfeiting to Switzerland's Roger Federer.

2014 was an unforgettable year for him, both professionally and personally, including his wedding and the birth of his first child. By winning his second Wimbledon, four *Masters 1000* (Indian Wells, Miami, Rome and Paris-Bercy) and the end-of-season Masters and finishing as the world's number one player, he enters a little more among the legends of tennis .

2015 - Historic season: 2ᵉ Petit Slam (Melbourne, Wimbledon, US Open), 5ᵉ Masters, record number of Masters 1000 titles in one season and record ATP points

For the first time in his career, Novak starts his official season with the Doha tournament. After two easy rounds against Dušan Lajović (6-2, 6-1) and Serhiy Stakhovsky (6-2, 6-1), he stops in the quarterfinals, beaten by the Croatian Ivo Karlović (7-6^2 , 6^6 -7, 4-6).

Novak enters the Australian Open as one of the favourites to win the world number one ranking and four titles in Melbourne. He easily reached the third round, defeating Slovenia's Aljaž Bedene (6-3, 6-2, 6-4) and Russia's Andrey Kuznetsov (6-0, 6-1, 6-4). He then faces former top 10 player and 2009 semifinalist Fernando Verdasco of Spain. Although a more dangerous opponent, Verdasco was easily eliminated by Novak with a score of 7-6^8 , 6-3, 6-4. The Serbian then qualified for the quarter-finals by eliminating Gilles Müller of Luxembourg (6-4, 7-5, 7-5). He then defeated Canada's Milos Raonic (7-6^5 , 6-4, 6-2) after a perfectly executed match, and then his opponent from the previous year, Switzerland's Stanislas Wawrinka (7-6^1 , 3-6, 6-4, 4-6, 6-0). Novak played his fifth Australian Open final against his rival Andy Murray, who had a perfect tournament, losing only two sets, the first in the round of 16 against Grigor Dimitrov and the second in the semifinals against Tomáš Berdych. He defeated the Briton in a match in which the first two sets were very intense, 7-6^5, 6^4 -7, 6-3, 6-0, becoming the first player in the Open Era to win this tournament five times, but remaining behind Roy Emerson (six titles). This 8^e career Grand Slam title also allows him to equal Andre Agassi, Jimmy Connors, Ivan Lendl, Fred Perry and Ken Rosewall in the number of Grand Slams won.

He made his return to competition at the Dubai Open. He reached the final by beating Tomáš Berdych in the semi-finals, but lost to Roger Federer (6-3, 7-5).

He participated in the first round of Davis Cup against Croatia and allowed Serbia to qualify for the quarterfinals after his singles win against Mate Delić in 3 sets (6-3, 6-2, 6-4) and his doubles win with Nenad Zimonjić.

Novak then travels to California to play the first Masters 1000 of the season, the Indian Wells Masters. The defending champion, Novak met little resistance until the final. He successively eliminated Márcos Baghdatís (6-1, 6-3), Albert Ramos (7-5, 6-3), John Isner (6-4, 7-6^5) and took advantage of the withdrawal of Australian Bernard Tomic to reach the semi-finals. He then eliminated Great Britain's Andy Murray in a one-sided match (6-2, 6-3) and qualified for a fifth final in the Californian desert. In a 38^e confrontation, Novak takes his revenge on the Swiss Roger Federer, whom he had not beaten since the 2014 Wimbledon tournament. This victory 6-3, 6^5 -7, 6-2 brings the Serb his second title of the season and the fiftieth of his career. From the following week, he travels to Miami, Florida, to participate in this unmissable *Masters 1000*. This year, he is still in the running to complete the Indian Wells - Miami double. He started off against Martin Kližan of Slovakia, whom he defeated 6-0, 5-7, 6-1, and then went on to defeat Steve Darcis (6-0, 7-5) in his second round match. In his next match against Ukrainian Alexandr Dolgopolov, he was almost eliminated. After being down 6^3 -7, 1-4, his opponent even had double-break points, he managed to turn the tables in the second set, and then won the decisive set after his opponent's physical breakdown, with a score of 6^3 -7, 7-5, 6-0. After that, he defeated David Ferrer (7-5, 7-5) and then the American giant John Isner (7-6^3 , 6-2) in the semifinals. He wins for the fifth time in his career in this tournament against Andy Murray in a match of high intensity (7-6^3 , 4-6, 6-0). He became the first player in the history of tennis to complete a triple Indian Wells-Miami double.

He then began the Monte Carlo Masters, which marked the start of the European clay court season, by eliminating Spain's Albert Ramos (6-1, 6-4), Austria's Andreas Haider-Maurer (6-4, 6-0) and Croatia's Marin Čilić (6-0, 6-3) to reach the semifinals. Novak scores his tenth 6-0 in the match against Marin Čilić in April. He then eliminates, in a 43^e confrontation, his great rival, the Spaniard Rafael Nadal (6-3, 6-3) to qualify for a fourth final in the principality. He won his second title in this tournament against Czech Tomáš Berdych (7-5, 4-6, 6-3), in a close match with ups and downs, and thus became the first player in tennis history to win the first three *Masters 1000* of a season, namely Indian Wells,

Miami and Monte Carlo . At the beginning of May, Novak decided not to participate in the Madrid Masters, in order to feel as good as possible for his goal, the French Open. In° his last preparatory tournament before the Paris Grand Slam, in Rome, he started with a difficult victory against Nicolás Almagro (6-1, 6^5 -7, 6-3), and then also defeated the Brazilian Thomaz Bellucci (5-7, 6-2, 6-3), and then eliminated in the quarterfinals the world number 5 Kei Nishikori by dropping another set (6-3, 3-6, 6-1). He defeated David Ferrer in a good match (6-4, 6-4), then in the final, he won another title by beating Roger Federer (6-4, 6-3). Before Roland Garros, he thus remains on a 22-match winning streak, and is undefeated in all major tournaments he has participated in since October 2014.

On May 22, during the draw for the Paris Grand Slam, he found himself in the same draw as the non-winner of the tournament Rafael Nadal and thus faced him in a clash that everyone expected from the quarterfinals, and this because the Spaniard is for the first time in this tournament outside the first four seeds. To begin his tournament, he eliminated Jarkko Nieminen (6-2, 7-5, 6-2), Gilles Müller (6-1, 6-4, 6-4) and the young Australian hopeful Thanasi Kokkinakis (6-4, 6-4, 6-4) in the first three rounds. He then gave Richard Gasquet a lesson (6-1, 6-2, 6-3). He easily reached the quarter-finals (only 36 games played in 4 matches) and defeated the non-winner of the Parisian tournament in 3 sets (7-5, 6-3, 6-1) with a great match, becoming the second man to beat Rafael Nadal on clay in 3 sets (after Robin Söderling in 2009). He also became the only player to have beaten Nadal at least once in all four Grand Slam tournaments. He then won for the third time in his career a place in the final of the Paris tournament by eliminating Andy Murray (6-3, 6-3, 5-7, 5-7, 6-1) in a tense match where he led two sets to zero. On June 7, 2015, he lost in the final to Stanislas Wawrinka (6-4, 4-6, 3-6, 4-6). After the match, he recognized the superiority of the Swiss and explained that it "was not his day".

As in previous years, he decided not to participate in any grass court tournament before Wimbledon. He easily reached the fourth round by eliminating Germany's Philipp Kohlschreiber (6-4, 6-4, 6-4), Finland's Jarkko Nieminen (6-4, 6-2, 6-3), who was playing the last Wimbledon of his career, and Australian Bernard Tomic (6-3, 6-3, 6-3). He then eliminated, during a very complicated match, spread over two days, the South African Kevin Anderson, seeded n° 14 (6^6 -7, 6^6 -7, 6-1, 6-4, 7-5). For a 25[e] consecutive Grand Slam quarterfinal, he eliminates, for the second time this season, Croatia's Marin Čilić (6-4, 6-4, 6-4). He then qualified for a third final in London by eliminating Frenchman Richard Gasquet (7-6^2 , 6-4, 6-4) in the semifinals. There he faced, for the fortieth time, the Swiss Roger Federer whom he beat 7-6^1 , 6^{10} -7, 6-4, 6-3 in two hours and fifty-six minutes. This victory brings his number of Grand Slam victories to nine, his number of Wimbledon victories to three (he equals the number of victories of his coach, Boris Becker), and marks his twentieth victory over Federer.

He begins the summer hard court season with the Canadian Masters, held this year in Montreal. He easily reached the quarter-finals by eliminating Brazilian Thomaz Bellucci (6-3, 7-6^4) and then American Jack Sock (6-2, 6-1). He then won a complicated match against the Latvian Ernests Gulbis (5-7, 7-6^7 , 6-1), despite a terrible season, saving two match points in the tie-break of the second set. He easily beat Jeremy Chardy (6-4, 6-4) in the semifinals. Despite being the favorite in the final against Andy Murray, he lost in three sets 4-6, 6-4, 3-6. His win-loss ratio increased to 52-4. He then enters the Cincinnati Masters, arguably the most important Masters of the season for Novak. Of the nine Masters 1000 events, this is the only one he has never won. He could become the first player to win all nine tournaments in his career. He reached the semi-finals with varying degrees of difficulty. He first defeated Frenchman Benoit Paire (7-5, 6-2), Belgian David Goffin 6-4, 2-6, 6-3, when he was down by a break in the last set, and Swiss Stanislas Wawrinka 6-4, 6-1. For the second time this season, he defeated Ukrainian Alexandr Dolgopolov (4-6, 7-6^5 , 6-2) to reach the final in pain. However, he lost to Roger Federer 6^1 -7, 3-6. These two defeats in tournaments where he was a favorite slightly erode his status as a favorite for the US Open.

At the US Open, he reached the fourth round by easily eliminating Brazilian João Souza (6-1, 6-1, 6-1), Austrian Andreas Haider-Maurer (6-4, 6-1, 6-2) and Italian Andreas Seppi (6-3, 7-5, 7-5). He defeated Spain's Roberto Bautista-Agut (6-3, 4-6, 6-4, 6-3), losing his first set of the tournament. He reached the semifinals again, defeating Spain's Feliciano Lopez (6-1, 3-6, 6-3, 7-6^2). He advances to the final by easily eliminating defending champion Marin Čilić (6-0, 6-1, 6-2), who was diminished by injury. In the final, he met his rival Roger Federer, as at Wimbledon, whom he once again defeated in four sets (6-4, 5-7, 6-4, 6-4). This final was particularly notable for the large number of break points saved by Novak, 19 out of 23. He thus enters the very closed circle of players who have won ten Grand Slam titles in a career. After this victory, in terms of the ATP ranking, he reached a record of 1,616,145 points and also achieved the largest gap ever between n° 1 and n° 2. He is also guaranteed to finish the year n° 1 in the world, for the fourth time in his career.

He then participated in the China Open, which he has already won 5 times and never lost. He easily reached the final, beating John Isner (6-2, 6-2) and David Ferrer in the semifinals (6-2, 6-3). There he met up with Rafael Nadal, whom he outclassed (6-2, 6-2) to win his 6^e title in the Chinese capital and sign an impressive 29-match unbeaten streak in Beijing, during which he only lost three sets. The following week, in Shanghai, the next round of the Asian tour, he started with a quick win against Martin Kližan (6-2, 6-1) and then defeated Feliciano López (6-2, 6-3). In the next round, after a tough first set, he defeated Bernard Tomic (7-6^6 , 6-1). By beating Tomic, he reached 13,645 points at the Race, making 2015 the year in which the Serbian won the most points, even better than in 2011 when he finished the year with 13,630 points. The next day, in a match in which he delivered a near-perfect performance, he outclassed Andy Murray (6-1, 6-3) and won a 13e consecutive final. In the final, he faced Jo-Wilfried Tsonga, a match he won (6-2, 6-4), thus equaling his 5e *Masters 1000* of the season, equaling his record of 2011 (co-held with Rafael Nadal in 2013). In addition, he becomes the record holder of titles in Shanghai with this third victory, and has an unprecedented 16,785 points in the ATP rankings on October 19. After this match, he himself admits that it is "the best year of his life".

In early November, he begins the year-end indoor season, a surface where he is undefeated since 2012. In the modernized and renamed AccorHotels Arena in Paris-Bercy, he started with a victory over Thomaz Bellucci (7-5, 6-3). He then eliminated Gilles Simon (6-3, 7-5) in a strange match with multiple breaks. The next day, he defeated Tomáš Berdych in a tough match (7-6^3 , 7-6^8). In 680 matches on the professional circuit, this is the first time he has won without breaking his opponent. In the semifinals, he met Stanislas Wawrinka. He won the first set but lost the second, ending his streak of 29 consecutive sets won. Nevertheless, he won the match in 3 sets (6-3, 3-6, 6-0). In the final, he plays Andy Murray for the 30e time in his career. He wins for the 3e consecutive times the Parisian tournament, a record. He also becomes the holder of the most titles in Paris-Bercy (4). With this victory, he set a new record of having won 6 out of 9 possible *Masters 1000 tournaments in* one season.

With this victory he reached a record of ATP Race points, namely 15,285 points.

In mid-November, he participated for the ninth consecutive time in the Masters tournament, where he is the three-time defending champion. He got off to a great start at the London Masters by beating Kei Nishikori (6-1, 6-1). He then met Roger Federer for the 43^e time. The Swiss won in two sets (7-5, 6-2) and put an end to a series of 38 consecutive victories on hard court in indoor for the Serb. However, he still qualified for the semifinals after defeating Tomáš Berdych (6-3, 7-5). He went on to defeat Spanish rival Rafael Nadal (6-3, 6-3) for the fourth time this season, earning a spot in the final against Roger Federer. By beating him (6-3, 6-4), he made history by becoming the only player to win four straight Masters titles at the end of the year. He concludes his year with the highest number of ATP points ever achieved at the end of the season: 16585 points. With 11 titles (three Grand Slams, the Masters, six Masters 1000, and one ATP 500), his season is among the greatest ever for a tennis player'' .

2016 - 2019: Grandeurs, injuries and return to the top

2016: 6ᵉ Australian Open, 1ᵉʳ French Open and Grand Slam over two seasons, finalist at US Open and Masters but lost 1ʳᵉ place

For the second year in a row, Novak Djokovic starts his season with the Doha tournament. He won his first match easily against the fantastic German Dustin Brown (6-2, 6-2), whom he was playing for the first time. He then defeated Fernando Verdasco by the same score, before facing Leonardo Mayer in the quarter-finals, whom he beat 6-3, 7-5. The next day, he defeated Tomáš Berdych (6-3, 7-6³) in the semi-finals. By reaching the final of this tournament, he has played in all the finals of the tournaments he has played in the last 52 weeks, 16 finals in as many tournaments played. He defeated Rafael Nadal (6-1, 6-2) in a match in which he played splendid tennis (30 winners and 13 unforced errors), and perfect from start to finish as he explained after the match, and thus won his 60ᵉ career title· . For the first time, he leads the head-to-head against Rafael Nadal with 24 wins in 47 meetings. He also improved his own ATP points record once again; he reached 16,790 ATP points.

The title holder in Melbourne, he began his campaign by beating the young South Korean Chung Hyeon in three sets (6-3, 6-2, 6-4). In the second round, he met another young player for the first time, the Frenchman Quentin Halys, whom he beat relatively easily despite a disputed final set (6-1, 6-2, 7-6[3]). In the third round, he met the Italian Andreas Seppi, seeded number 29, whom he also beat in three sets, two of which were close (6-1, 7-5, 7-6[6]). In the round of 16, he meets Gilles Simon, the match is very close, Novak wins the match in 5 sets (6-3, 6[1] -7, 6-4, 4-6, 6-3) but makes no less than 100 unforced errors, a first in his career. In the quarter-finals, he met up with Nippon's Kei Nishikori, against whom he had lost a Grand Slam match (US Open 2014). He won this match in 3 sets (6-3, 6-2, 6-4) and met again for a 45[e] confrontation with the Swiss Roger Federer. Djokovic, during this semi-final, produced a tennis of very high intensity during the first two sets, before a rebellion of the Swiss in the 3[e] . He finally won in 4 sets (6-1, 6-2, 3-6, 6-3) and for the first time in 45 duels, took the lead over the Swiss. He thus qualifies for his 6[e] final at the Australian Open, which he wins in three consecutive sets (6-1, 7-5, 7-6[3]) against the British and number 2 seed, Andy Murray, thus equaling the record of six victories in men's singles for this Grand Slam tournament held for almost fifty years (1967) by Australian Roy Emerson. He also equals Rod Laver and Björn Borg in the number of Grand Slam titles won[.] .

As usual, he resumes competition at the Dubai Open. This tournament is special, he can equal the record of Ivan Lendl dating from 1981-1982 who had chained 18 consecutive finals. In the first round, he met the Spaniard Tommy Robredo, whom he beat in two sets (6-1, 6-2). With this same score, he signs the 700[e] victory of his career by beating the Tunisian Malek

Jaziri. His streak of 17 consecutive finals ends in the next round, where after losing the first set 3-6 against Feliciano Lopez, he decides to quit due to an eye problem.

He participates in the first round of Davis Cup against Kazakhstan and allows Serbia to qualify for the quarterfinals after his 2 victories in singles against Aleksandr Nedovyesov in 3 sets (6-1, 6-2, 6-3) and Mikhail Kukushkin in a breathless match where Novak was not far from giving up because of a pain in his thigh, but wins the match in 5 sets (6^6 -7, 7-6^3 , 4-6, 6-3, 6-2).

During the American tour in March, in Indian Wells, he started against the young American Bjorn Fratangelo, who came from the qualifiers, which he beat in three sets (2-6, 6-2, 6-1). In the second round, he defeated Germany's Philipp Kohlschreiber (7-5, 7-5) and then took revenge on Feliciano Lopez in two sets (6-3, 6-3). In the quarter-finals, he met up with Jo-Wilfried Tsonga, whom he defeated in two tie-breaks (7-6^2 , 7-6^2) to join his eternal rival Rafael Nadal in the semi-finals for the 48th time[e] . After a balanced first set, he won (7-6^5 , 6-2) in 1 hour and 58 minutes to join Milos Raonic. He thus reaches his 3[e] final in a row in Indian Wells and also his 10[e] consecutive *Masters 1000* final since Paris-Bercy in 2014. The next day, in a match that was totally under his control, he outclassed Milos Raonic (6-2, 6-0), and thus became the record holder of titles in Indian Wells with 5 trophies in this tournament. It is also his 3rd[e] Indian Wells in a row and thus equals Roger

Federer's record. Finally, with this 27^e *Masters 1000* in his pocket, he becomes the co-holder with Rafael Nadal of the greatest number of titles in this category[,] . The following week, he starts the Miami Masters where he is the title holder. In the first round, he defeated the young British Kyle Edmund (6-3, 6-3) and then the Portuguese João Sousa in two sets (6-4, 6-1). He then faced the Austrian Dominic Thiem, whom he beat with difficulty in two sets that were more balanced than the score would suggest (6-3, 6-4), since he saved 14 break points out of 15. In the quarter-finals, he eliminated Czech Tomáš Berdych (6-3, 6-3) and joined Belgian David Goffin in the semi-finals, beating him in two tight sets (7-6^5 , 6-4). He reaches a 7^e consecutive *Masters 1000* final without missing a tournament and it is also the 11^e in a row since Paris-Bercy in 2014. In the final, he defeated Japan's Kei Nishikori in two sets (6-3, 6-3). With this victory, he becomes the record holder of titles in *Masters 1000* with 28 titles. He also equals Andre Agassi with 6 titles in Miami, it is his 3^e consecutive, two records shared with the American. It is also his 4^e Indian Wells-Miami double, including the 3^e in a row, which is also a record. With this victory, he has a lead of 8725 points over his runner-up Andy Murray, which is an unprecedented point difference between the two world leaders.

He starts the clay court season at home, at the Monte Carlo Masters where he is the defending champion. He lost his first match to Czech Jiří Veselý in 3 sets (4-6, 6-2, 4-6). This ends his streak of 11 consecutive *Masters 1000* finals and he is joined by Rafael Nadal who came back tied in the number of *Masters 1000* wins, after his victory in Monte Carlo. He returns to competition at the Madrid Masters, a tournament he has not played since 2013. In his first match, he faced for the first time the young and talented Borna Ćorić, whom he defeated without problems (6-2, 6-4). He then easily defeats Roberto Bautista-Agut with the score of (6-2, 6-1). In the quarter-finals, he meets the Canadian Milos Raonic whom he eliminates in two sets (6-3, 6-4). In the last four, Novak defeated Kei Nishikori (6-3, 7-6[4]) in a tightly contested match to reach his second final in Madrid, which he had not reached since 2011. He joined defending champion Andy Murray, whom he beat despite losing the second set (6-2, 3-6, 6-3). He becomes the only player to have won 8 *Masters 1000* at least twice. At the same time, he sets the record for the number of Masters 1000 victories, with 29 titles (compared to 28 for Rafael Nadal). The following week, he takes part in the Rome Masters. He played his first match against the Frenchman Stéphane Robert and won with difficulty in two sets (7-5, 7-5). In the next round, he met again, as he did the previous year at the same stage of the competition, the Brazilian Thomaz Bellucci. He struggled to get into his match and lost the first set 6-0, a first since his match against Roger Federer in Cincinnati in 2012. He still ends up winning the match in 3 sets (0-6, 6-3, 6-2). He will meet his biggest rival Rafael Nadal for the 49[e] time in his career. Despite the wind, Novak won in two tight sets (7-5, 7-6[4]) in 2h24 and won his 7[e] match in a row against the Spaniard. The next day, he defeated Japanese Kei

Nishikori in a breathtaking match lasting more than 3 hours. He won in three sets (2-6, 6-4, 7-6^5) and reached a 42^e *Masters 1000* final, equaling the record of Roger Federer and Rafael Nadal. For the second time in a week, he faced the British Andy Murray in the final of a *Masters 1000*. He lost in two sets (3-6, 3-6), the first time since 2004 that a winner in Rome is other than the Serb or Rafael Nadal.

At the French Open, Novak Djokovic set out to win his first Parisian title and a two-year Grand Slam. He won his first three matches in three sets against Lu Yen-hsun (6-4, 6-1, 6-1), Steve Darcis (7-5, 6-3, 6-4) and Aljaž Bedene (6-2, 6-3, 6-3). In the round of 16, he defeated Spain's Roberto Bautista-Agut in four sets (3-6, 6-4, 6-1, 7-5) in two days of difficult weather conditions. He thus qualifies for his 36^e Grand Slam quarterfinals, the 28^e in a row. He then defeated Tomáš

Berdych in three sets (6-3, 7-5, 6-3) to reach his 30[es] Grand Slam semifinals. In the semifinals, he defeated the young Austrian Dominic Thiem (6-2, 6-1, 6-4) to reach his fourth Porte d'Auteuil final. This is[e] his 6th consecutive Grand Slam final. He found Andy Murray, his runner-up in the world rankings, and dominated him in four sets (3-6, 6-1, 6-2, 6-4). This victory makes him the fifth player in the Open Era to win all four Grand Slams, and the eighth in tennis history. He has now won a Grand Slam in two seasons, something only two men have done in their careers before him: Donald Budge in 1937-1938 (outside of the Open Era), and Rod Laver in his calendar Grand Slams of 1962 and 1969. Djokovic is however the first in history to do so on three different surfaces, the 4 Grand Slams still being played at the time of Laver all on grass or clay. He also set the record for the highest total of ATP points by a singles player, with 16,950 points. He is the first player since Jim Courier in 1992 to win the first two Grand Slams of the year, before Wimbledon, the Rio Olympics and the US Open. At this point he remains in contention for a *golden Grand Slam in* a year.

However, on July 2, after two matches won in three sets, he was prematurely defeated in the third round of Wimbledon, against American Sam Querrey (6[6] -7, 1-6, 6-3, 6[5] -7), in a two-day match stopped several times by rain. The match was stopped several times by the rain. He reached the round of 16 for the first time in a Grand Slam since the 2009 French Open, ending a streak of 30 consecutive major tournament wins.

He resumed competition on July 27 at the Rogers Cup. He defeated Gilles Müller in two tight sets (7-5, 7-6^3), and the next day he defeated Czech Radek Štěpánek more easily (6-2, 6-4). In the quarterfinals, he met Tomáš Berdych for the 27^e time, whom he eliminated with difficulty, saving three first set points (7-6^6 , 6-4). In the semifinals, he easily defeated Gaël Monfils in two sets (6-3, 6-2) and qualified for the 43^e final of his career in the *Masters 1000*, which is a new record, surpassing the 42 finals reached by Rafael Nadal and Roger Federer. He won the title by beating Kei Nishikori in two sets (6-3, 7-5), thus winning his 30^e *Masters 1000*, and his 4^e title in Canada.

During the Olympic Games, where he had great ambitions to win a gold medal, he had a difficult first round against Juan Martin del Potro, who was returning from injury. The Argentine beat him in two sets in the decisive games (6^4 -7, 6^2 -7), giving him a big disappointment. He also plays doubles with his compatriot Nenad Zimonjić and loses in the second round to the Brazilian pair of Marcelo Melo and Bruno Soares (6-4, 6-4). With a wrist injury, he decided to take a break before the US Open and forfeited Cincinnati as the only *Masters 1000 event* missing from the Serbian's record.

Uncertain about the condition of his wrist, he starts the US Open by facing for the first time the Polish Jerzy Janowicz, whom he beats in 4 sets (6-3, 5-7, 6-2, 6-1). He passed the second round without playing thanks to the forfeit of the Czech Jiří Veselý, and then the 3^e after only 6 games (4-2 in his favor) against Mikhail Youzhny, forced to withdraw due to a knee injury. In the next round, he plays the young British Kyle Edmund, whom he beats in 3 sets (6-2, 6-1, 6-4), in the quarterfinals he plays for the first time in New York Jo-Wilfried Tsonga with whom he plays only 2 sets (6-3, 6-2, ab.), Tsonga having to withdraw due to an injury to his left leg. Tsonga's withdrawal makes Djokovic the first player in the Open Era to reach the semifinals, benefiting from three withdrawals or forfeits from his opponents. He[ee] reached his 10th consecutive semifinal in New York against Gaël Monfils, whom he defeated in four sets in a razor-thin match (6-3, 6-2, 3-6, 6-2). He then reached his seventh final at the US Open, the 21st[e] in a Grand Slam, where he faced Stanislas Wawrinka, who defeated Kei Nishikori in four sets. In the final, he lost to Stanislas Wawrinka who, after losing the first set, recovered to win the next three (6^1 -7, 6-4, 7-5, 6-3).

To everyone's surprise, Novak Djokovic decides to withdraw from the China Open, a tournament he has already won six times, preferring to train in his hometown Belgrade. During his stay in Serbia he declares that since his title at Roland Garros he has lost the taste to take pleasure in playing tennis because of the pressure to chase records and titles. He decided not to set any more goals for himself but to enjoy being on the court again. He resumed competition at the Shanghai Masters, in the first round he easily defeated the Italian Fabio Fognini in two sets (6-3, 6-3), then the Canadian Vasek Pospisil in two sets (6-4, 6-4) and the German Mischa Zverev from the qualifiers, whom he defeated with difficulty in three sets (3-6, 7-6^4 , 6-3). However, he lost in the semifinals against the Spaniard Roberto Bautista-Agut against whom he lost in two sets (6-4, 6-4) leaving Andy Murray to catch up with him in the race for the world number 1. Engaged in Paris Bercy, a tournament in which he remains on three consecutive wins, the Serb starts with a victory in two sets (6-3, 6-4) against Gilles Müller. He then struggled to get past Grigor Dimitrov in three sets (4-6, 6-2, 6-3) and fell in the quarterfinals to an excellent Marin Cilic, an opponent he had never lost to, in two sets (6-4, 7-6^2). He will lose his place as world number 1. Qualified for the Masters, Djokovic inherited a pool including Gael Monfils, Dominic Thiem and Milos Raonic, three opponents against whom he had never lost. This figure is verified as he wins all three of his matches. He beat Thiem in three sets (6-7^{10} , 6-0, 6-2), Raonic in two (7-6^6 , 7-6^5), and Monfils forfeited his last match. He then faced David Goffin (against whom he had never lost), whom he beat in two sets (6-2, 6-1). Qualified for the semifinals, he meets Kei Nishikori as in 2014. And as in 2015, in pool play, he beats him by a score of 6-1, 6-1. Despite two good last matches, he does not find his level in the final against Andy Murray. He loses in two sets (6-3, 6-4). He will end the year number 2 for the first time since 2013. The year also ends with the announcement of the end of the collaboration with his coach Boris Becker, who points to the lack of work of the Serb and highlights the rapprochement of Djokovic with Pepe Imaz (en), a mental coach sometimes described as "guru", controversial creator of an "academy" professing the sport by "love and peace". According to Pepe Imaz, Djokovic's priority is not to be number 1 in the world, but to focus on his well-being.

2017: Season without major title cut short due to elbow injury, out of top 10

Novak Djokovic starts his season with the tournament in Qatar where he is the title holder. For his first outing of the year he plays the German Jan-Lennard Struff whom he beats in 2 sets (7-6^1 , 6-3) after being down 5-1 in the first set. He then defeats the Argentine Horacio Zeballos and the Czech Radek Štěpánek in 2 sets (6-3, 6-4) and (6-3, 6-3). In the semifinals he meets the Spaniard Fernando Verdasco whom he beats in 3 sets (4-6, 7-6^7 , 6-3) after saving five match points. In the final, he met the world's number one player Andy Murray for the 36^e time, whom he defeated after an intense final of 2 hours and 53 minutes in three sets (6-3, 5-7, 6-4). After more than five months without a title, Novak Djokovic wins the 67^e title of his career. It also puts an end to a series of 28 consecutive victories by the Scot.

At the Australian Open, he lost in the second round to the 117^e Denis Istomin (6^8 -7, 7-5, 6-2, 6^5 -7, 4-6). This is the first time since 2006 that he lost before the round of 16 in Australia.

He participates in the 1er round of Davis Cup in the city of Niš in Serbia against Russia and beats Daniil Medvedev on withdrawal (3-6, 6-4, 6-1, 1-0 ab.). Serbia qualified for the quarterfinals.

For the first time he decides to participate in the Acapulco tournament. He won his first round match in two sets against Martin Kližan (6-3, 7-6^4) and then faced the Argentine Juan Martín del Potro in the second round. He defeated him in three sets (4-6, 6-3, 6-4) after a tough battle and two and a half hours of play. In the next round, Nick Kyrgios pulled off a shocking upset, defeating him in two tight sets (6^9 -7, 5-7). In the Indian Wells tournament, where he is a three-time defending champion, he met Juan Martin del Potro in the third round and defeated the Argentine in three sets (7-5, 4-6, 6-1), before Nick Kyrgios defeated him again (4-6, 6^3 -7) in one hour and 54 minutes.

In April, after recovering from an elbow injury that forced him to miss the Miami Masters, he joined the Serbian Davis Cup team to play the quarterfinals against Spain, which was without its top players Rafael Nadal and Roberto Bautista-Agut. He gave Serbia a 1-0 lead with his easy win over Albert Ramos-Viñolas (6-3, 6-4, 6-2) and advanced to the semifinals.

He starts the season on clay in Monte-Carlo. For his debut, he won a tough 2:31 match against Frenchman Gilles Simon, who served for the match at 5-4 in the 3^e set (6-3, 3-6, 7-5). He then defeated Pablo Carreño Busta (6-2, 4-6, 6-4) before losing to David Goffin (2-6, 6-3, 5-7). Just before the Madrid tournament, Djokovic announced the end of his collaboration with his coach, Marián Vajda, his physical trainer Gebhard Phil-Gritsch, and his physiotherapist Miljan Amanovic. In Madrid, he defeated Nicolás Almagro in three sets and then Feliciano López in two sets to advance to the quarterfinals; benefiting from Kei Nishikori's forfeit, he reached the semifinals where he met Rafael Nadal for the 50^e time, who defeated him soundly (6-2, 6-4). The following week, he played in Rome. Until the final, he did not lose a set, beating successively Aljaž Bedene (7-6^2 , 6-2), Roberto Bautista-Agut (6-4, 6-4), Juan Martin del Potro (6-1, 6-4), and Dominic Thiem (6-1, 6-0). In the final, he met the young German prodigy Alexander Zverev who defeated him 6-4, 6-3.

He starts Roland Garros with his new coach Andre Agassi. He passes the first rounds by beating Marcel Granollers (6-3, 6-4, 6-2), João Sousa (6-1, 6-4, 6-3) and Diego Schwartzman who takes 2 sets (5-7, 6-3, 3-6, 6-1, 6-1). In the round of 16, he defeated Albert Ramos-Viñolas (7-6^5 , 6-1, 6-3) and then was beaten for the first time in the quarter by Dominic Thiem (6^5 -7, 3-6, 0-6). It was his first 6-0 loss in a Grand Slam since the 2005 US Open, and a match against Gaël Monfils that he eventually won.

He decided to enter the Eastbourne tournament as a wild card to prepare for Wimbledon. This is the first time since 2010 that he enters a tournament a week before the start of a Grand Slam. He defeated Vasek Pospisil (6-4, 6-3), Donald Young (6-2, 7-6^9) and Daniil Medvedev (6-4, 6-4) to reach his 98^e final on the professional circuit. He won his 68^e ATP title by beating Gaël Monfils in two sets (6-3, 6-4).

He began Wimbledon by winning his first match against Martin Kližan (6-3, 2-0 ab.), then defeated Czech Adam Pavlásek (6-2, 6-2, 6-1), Latvian Ernests Gulbis (6-4, 6-1, 7-6^2) and Frenchman Adrian Mannarino (6-2, 7-6^4 ,

6-3) in the round of 16. He joined Czech Tomáš Berdych in the quarter-finals against whom he was forced to retire (6-7^2 , 2-0 ab.), following an elbow injury that has been bothering him for several months. In order to treat his injury, he decided at the end of July to end his season. After 50 consecutive Grand Slam appearances, he ended this streak by forgoing the US Open. This is the first season since 2010 that he has not won a Grand Slam title and since 2006 that he has not reached a semi-final.

He finished the year outside the top 10, for the first time since 2007, in 12th place, with two ATP 250 titles.

2018 : Difficult start to the season, 4^e Wimbledon, 3^e US Open, Career Golden Masters and No. 1 at the end of the season

For the year 2018, Novak Djokovic announced on 1er December 2017 continue the adventure with Andre Agassi but also added Radek Štěpánek in his staff.

Djokovic was announced for the Mubadala World Tennis Championship and the Doha Open, where he is the defending champion, but he was forced to withdraw after feeling pain in his elbow during training.

After participating in the Kooyong exhibition, he starts the Australian Open by beating Donald Young in the first round in 3 sets (6-1, 6-2, 6-4) and then gets rid of Gaël Monfils in 4 sets (4-6, 6-3, 6-1, 6-3) while the temperature reaches 40 degrees. This is his 15^e win in a row against the French player, against whom he has not suffered any defeat. He then easily defeated Spain's Albert Ramos-Viñolas (6-2, 6-3, 6-3) but was eliminated in the round of 16 (7-6⁴ , 7-5, 7-6³) by the young South Korean Chung Hyeon, who plays a style of play similar to his own.

On the advice of Radek Štěpánek he decided to undergo a minor operation on his elbow which made his return to the circuit uncertain.

Uncertain for Indian Wells, he finally decides to take part and plays Taro Daniel for his first match, against whom he loses in three sets (7-6³ , 4-6, 6-1), physically breaking down at the end of the match. He decides to enter the Miami Masters where he plays Benoit Paire, but loses in two sets (6-3, 6-4). He then parted ways with his coaches Andre Agassi and Radek Štěpánek.

Shortly before the start of the clay court season, he met up with his long-time coach, Marian Vajda, with whom he won all his major titles. Vajda asked Novak to exclude Pepe Imaz from his coaching staff and asked him to eat more protein because the Spanish guru had forbidden him to eat anything other than vegetables. With the Slovak in his staff, he starts his season on ochre at the Monte Carlo Masters where he severely beats Dušan Lajović (6-0, 6-1) in the first round. In the second round, he defeats Borna Ćorić (7-6^2, 7-5), on his 10^e match point, and is then beaten by Dominic Thiem in 3 sets (7-6^2, 2-6, 3-6). He receives an invitation to play in the Barcelona tournament. He is defeated by Martin Kližan of Slovakia in his first match (2-6, 6-1, 3-6). In the Madrid Masters, he defeated Kei Nishikori in the first round (7-5, 6-4) but lost in the second round to Kyle Edmund (6-3, 2-6, 6-3). In Rome, he started by beating Alexandr Dolgopolov in two sets (6-1, 6-3) and Nikoloz Basilashvili (6-4, 6-2) and then eliminated Kei Nishikori after a long, intense match lasting two hours and 21 minutes in three sets (2-6, 6-1, 6-3). In the semifinals, he met Rafael Nadal who beat him for the 25e time (7-6,^{4}, 6-3) and found himself at 22e in the world ranking, outside the top 20 for the first time since October 2006.

At the French Open, he won his first two matches against the Brazilian Rogério Dutra Silva in three sets (6-3, 6-4, 6-4) and then against the young Spaniard Jaume Munar (7-6^1 , 6-4, 6-4). He reached the quarterfinals by beating Roberto Bautista-Agut in four sets (6-4, 6^6 -7, 7-6^4 , 6-2) in the third round and Fernando Verdasco in three sets (6-3, 6-4, 6-2) in the round of 16. He was defeated by the amazing Italian Marco Cecchinato (3-6, 6^4 -7, 6-1, 6^{11} -7).

After having doubts about the season on grass, he finally decided to return to Queen's, a tournament he had not played since 2010. He won his first match against Australian John Millman in two sets (6-2, 6-1) and then defeated Grigor Dimitrov, the number 2 seed, 6-4, 6-1. This is the first member of the top 10 that Djokovic has beaten since the Rome Masters 1000 in 2017. He then defeated two Frenchmen Adrian Mannarino (7-5, 6-1) and Jeremy Chardy (7-6^5 , 6-1) to play the 99^e final of his career. This is actually the first final he has played in nearly a year, the last being during the Eastbourne tournament in June 2017. He also reached the 800^e victory on the professional circuit which puts him in the prestigious ranking of players who have won at least 800 matches. He eventually lost to Marin Čilić in 3 sets (7-5, 6^4 -7, 3-6).

At Wimbledon he is seeded number 12 and plays his first match against the American Tennys Sandgren whom he easily beats (6-3, 6-1, 6-2). He then successively defeated Argentine Horacio Zeballos (6-1, 6-2, 6-3) and British Kyle Edmund, seeded 21, in four sets (4-6, 6-3, 6-2, 6-4). In the round of 16 he faced for the first time the Russian Karen Khachanov whom he defeated in three sets (6-4, 6-2, 6-2) to reach the quarterfinals of a Grand Slam for the 41^e time. He eliminates Japanese Kei Nishikori (6-3, 3-6, 6-2, 6-2) qualifying for his first Grand Slam semifinal since the 2016 US Open. In indoor conditions, he then defeated his great rival Rafael Nadal, after a dantesque and very close match in 5h15 of play over two days, 6-4, 3-6, 7-6^9 , 3-6, 10-8, to earn the right to play a 5^e final at Wimbledon. He wins his 4^e Wimbledon trophy by easily beating South African Kevin Anderson in 3 sets (6-2, 6-2, 7-6^3). This is his first Grand Slam win since the French Open in 2016 and the 13^e of his career being only one behind Pete Sampras. This tournament allows him to return to the top 10 that he left in November 2017.

He resumed competition at the Rogers Cup. In the first round, he defeated the Bosnian lucky loser Mirza Bašić in two sets (6-3, 7-6^3), and then more easily got rid of the Canadian Peter Polansky (6-2, 6-4). In the round of 16, he met for the first time the young Greek Stéfanos Tsitsipás, a rising star of tennis against whom he lost in three sets (3-6, 7-6^5 , 3-6). In Cincinnati, he went on to win the only *Masters 1000 title* missing from his record. He defeats American Steve Johnson in two sets (6-4, 7-6^4) and then Frenchman Adrian Mannarino in three sets (4-6, 6-2, 6-1). Due to bad weather, he played the round of 16 and quarterfinal matches on the same day, beating Bulgaria's Grigor Dimitrov and then Canadian Milos Raonic in three sets (2-6, 6-3, 6-4) and (7-5, 4-6,

6-3). He then defeats Marin Čilić in the semifinals in three sets (6-4, 3-6, 6-3) to reach his 6[e] final in Cincinnati and the 45[e] in *Masters 1000*. He met again in the final Roger Federer after more than two years without playing each other, whom he beat in two sets (6-4, 6-4) winning for the first time this tournament. He becomes the first player to have won at least once each of these tournaments in singles since their inception in 1990 accomplishing a *Career Golden Masters*.

He won his first match at the 2018 US Open against Hungary's Márton Fucsovics in 4 sets (6-3, 3-6, 6-4, 6-0) in difficult weather conditions. He then defeats American Tennys Sandgren also in 4 sets (6-1, 6-3, 6^2 - 7, 6-2) and then consecutively beats Frenchman Richard Gasquet and Portuguese João Sousa in three sets, respectively (6-2, 6-3, 6-3) and (6-3, 6-4, 6-3). He reached his 42[e] quarter-finals in Grand Slam and became the second player with the most quarter-finals in this category behind Federer (53) and ahead of Jimmy Connors (41). He defeated the surprising John Millman in three sets (6-3, 6-4, 6-4), the surprise winner in the previous round of Roger Federer, to reach the semifinals in Grand Slam for the 33[e] time. In the semifinals, he easily defeated Japan's Kei Nishikori (6-3, 6-4, 6-2) to reach the 23[e] career Grand Slam final and the 8[e] at the US Open, a record he shares with Pete Sampras and Ivan Lendl. He won the final of the tournament, beating Juan Martin del Potro in three sets (6-3, $7\text{-}6^4$, 6-3), winning his third[e] US Open and his 14[e] Grand Slam title, equaling his idol Pete Sampras. With this victory he returns to the top 5 of the ATP rankings, one year after leaving it.

After participating in the Laver Cup, an unofficial competition, he entered the Shanghai Masters during the Asian tour. In his first match, he defeated Frenchman Jeremy Chardy in two sets (6-3, 7-5) without conceding a break point, and then Italian Marco Cecchinato, his opponent at the French Open, in two sets (6-4, 6-0). He[o] then defeated South Africa's Kevin Anderson in two sets (7-6[1], 6-3), before earning a spot in the final for the 46[e] time in this category after beating world No. 5 Alexander Zverev for the first time in two sets (6-2, 6-1). He is thus assured of taking the number two spot in the world from Roger Federer at the end of the tournament. In the final, he defeats the young Croatian Borna Ćorić in two sets (6-3, 6-4) and thus wins for the 4[e] time the Shanghai Masters and its 32[e] *Masters 1000* and comes within one unit of the record of titles held by Rafael Nadal in this category. He won this title without losing a set and without being broken, a performance achieved only by Roger Federer and Alexander Zverev in this category before.

He did not return to competition until the Paris-Bercy Masters, where he defeated João Sousa of Portugal in two sets (7-5, 6-1). Following Rafael Nadal's withdrawal the next day, this victory ensures his return to the number one spot in the world, two years after losing it to Andy Murray. He then successively defeats the Bosnian Damir Džumhur after his withdrawal in the second set (6-1, 2-1 ab.) and the Croatian Marin Čilić against whom he loses his first set since the second round of the US Open with the score of (4-6, 6-2, 6-3). In the semifinals he meets for the 47^e time the Swiss Roger Federer whom he beats in a breathless and undecided match in three sets (7-6^6 , 5-7, 7-6^3) to reach his 47^e final in *Masters 1000*. He lost the final to the young Russian Karen Khachanov, ending his streak of 22 consecutive wins since the US Open.

Before the start of the Masters, Rafael Nadal puts a definitive end to his season, ensuring that Novak Djokovic finishes the year as world number one for the 5^e time in his career. He equals Jimmy Connors and Roger Federer with only Pete Sampras left. He becomes the only tennis player to finish as world number one at the end of the year having been outside the top 20 during the season· . At the Masters, he won his first match against American John Isner in two sets (6-4, 6-3), then won his second match against German Alexander Zverev in two sets (6-4, 6-1) and finally won his last pool match against Marin Čilić in two sets (7-6^7 , 6-2) achieving a no contest. In the semifinals he defeats South African Kevin Anderson in two sets (6-2, 6-2) to reach the 7^e final at the Masters in his career. While he is on a streak of 40 service games won in a row and only 3 break points to save in the whole tournament, he can't find a solution against Alexander Zverev and loses the final (4-6, 3-6).

2019: 7ᵉ record title at the Australian Open, 5ᵉ Wimbledon, 2 Masters 1000 titles and loss of 1ʳᵉ world ranking

Novak Djokovic begins the 2019 season by participating in the exhibition of the Mubadala World Tennis Championship, which he wins for the 4ᵉ time by beating Russia's Karen Khachanov in two sets (6-4, 6-2), then South Africa's Kevin Anderson in three sets (4-6, 7-5, 7-5). For his first official tournament of the season in Doha, he began the tournament with an easy win over Damir Džumhur (6-1, 6-2), then beat Márton Fucsovics (4-6, 6-4, 6-1) and Nikoloz Basilashvili (4-6, 6-3, 6-4) with more difficulty in three sets. He was eliminated in the semi-finals by Roberto Bautista-Agut (6-3, 6⁶ -7, 4-6). He also reached the semi-finals in doubles with his brother Marko Djokovic where they were stopped by Pierre-Hugues Herbert and David Goffin (1-6, 6-3, 13-15).

Novak Djokovic began his 15ᵉ Australian Open with a three-set victory in the first round over American qualifier Mitchell Krueger (6-3, 6-2, 6-2) and dominated Frenchman Jo-Wilfried Tsonga in the second round, also in three sets (6-3, 7-5, 6-4). ᵉIn the third round, he played for the first time against the young Canadian prodigy Denis Shapovalov whom he defeated in four sets after a break in the third set (6-3, 6-4, 4-6, 6-0). In the round of 16, he defeated Russian Daniil Medvedev in four sets (6-4, 6⁵ -7, 6-2, 6-3) in a very physical match that allowed him to reach the quarter-finals of a Grand Slam tournament for the 43ᵉ time, where he defeated Japan's Kei Nishikori (6-1, 4-1 ab.), thus reaching the 34[e] semifinals of his Grand Slam career. In the semifinals, he defeated Frenchman Lucas Pouille in three sets (6-0, 6-2, 6-2), playing one of the best matches of his career, and met again with Rafael Nadal in the final for their 53[e] confrontation, the second in Australia. He defeated the Spaniard in three sets (6-3, 6-2, 6-3) in a controlled match and won the Australian Open for the 7[e] time, becoming the tournament's only record holder and his 15[e] Grand Slam tournament. He became the first player to beat Rafael Nadal in three sets in a Grand Slam final and also the only player to win three Grand Slam tournaments in a row three times, Roger Federer having done it twice.

After a disappointing American tour where he did not reach the quarter-finals in either Indian Wells or Miami, he began the clay court season in Monte Carlo. He reached the quarter-finals where he was eliminated by Russian Daniil Medvedev (14[e] world player) in three sets (6-3, 4-6, 6-2). At the Madrid Masters, he defeated American Taylor Fritz and Frenchman Jeremy Chardy in two sets (6-4, 6-2) and (6-1, 7-6[2]) to reach his 79e quarterfinals in this category. Qualifying directly for the semifinals after the withdrawal of Croatian Marin Čilić, he defeats Austrian Dominic Thiem in two sets (7-6[2] , 7-6[4]) to advance to his 48e Masters 1000 final against young Greek Stéfanos Tsitsipás. He won the final in two sets (6-3, 6-4) to claim his 3e title in Madrid and become the joint-record holder of 33 Masters 1000 titles with Rafael Nadal. At the Rome Masters, he defeated Canadian Denis Shapovalov in two sets (6-1, 6-3), then

German Philipp Kohlschreiber (6-3, 6-0), before meeting up with Argentine Juan Martin del Potro, whom he defeated in three sets and more than three hours of play (4-6, 7-6[6] , 6-4) after saving two match points in the tie-break of the second set. He advances to the 49[e] Masters 1000 final of his career by beating Diego Schwartzman in three sets (6-3, 6-7[2] , 6-3) and meets Rafael Nadal for the 54[e] confrontation of their careers. He was defeated by his great rival with the score of (6-0, 4-6, 6-1) which let the Majorcan regain the lead in the number of titles in Masters 1000.

Novak Djokovic enters the French Open as the world's No. 1 player and the holder of three previous Grand Slam titles (Wimbledon and US Open 2018, Australian Open 2019). Seeded No.° 1, he is one of the favorites along with clay court specialists Rafael Nadal and Dominic Thiem. He won his first three matches without dropping a set against Hubert Hurkacz (6-4, 6-2, 6-2), Henri Laaksonen (6-1, 6-4, 6-3) and Salvatore Caruso (6-3, 6-3, 6-2) and advanced to the round of 16 where he met German Jan-Lennard Struff, ranked 45[e] on the ATP, whom he beat soundly in three sets and 1 hour 33 minutes (6-3, 6-3, 6-2). For° his 44[e] Grand Slam quarter-final, postponed by one day due to weather conditions, he faced another German, the young Alexander Zverev, seeded No. 5 (7-5, 6-2, 6-2), whom he dominated in three sets and 2 hours and 9 minutes, despite a first set in which he saved a set point. This is[e] the first time he has reached a Grand Slam semifinal, where he will meet young Austrian Dominic Thiem, seeded No.° 4, one of the tournament's favorites. The match against Thiem was interrupted several times due to rain, with gusts of wind from storm Miguel adding difficulty to the game, and was played over two days on Friday, June 7 and Saturday, June 8. Thiem was able to get the better of Djokovic after many twists and turns over five hard-fought sets in 4 hours and 13 minutes (6-2, 3-6, 7-5, 5-7, 7-5). Djokovic showed his irritation with the referee on several occasions, notably after receiving a penalty for exceeding the 25-second time limit for the release of the serve.

Not participating in any official competition before Wimbledon, he defeated Germany's Philipp Kohlschreiber in three sets (6-3, 7-5, 6-3) and then the American Denis Kudla (6-3, 6-2, 6-2). He qualified for the round of 16 by beating Hubert Hurkacz of Poland in four sets (7-5,[5] 6-7, 6-1, 6-4) and then for the 45[e] Grand Slam quarter-finals of his career by beating the young Frenchman Ugo Humbert (6-3, 6-2, 6-3) He defeated David Goffin in the quarter-finals after a tight first set (6-4, 6-0, 6-2), then in the semifinals against Spain's Roberto Bautista-Agut, against whom he had already lost twice this season in a tight four-set match (6-2, 4-6, 6-3, 6-2). In the final, he meets Roger Federer for their 48[e] confrontation. After four hours and fifty-five minutes, the longest final in the history of Wimbledon, he won after saving two match points in the fifth set, and won his sixteenth Grand Slam tournament with the historic score of (7-6[5] , 1-6, 7-6[4] , 4-6, 13-12[3]). This is the first final in the history of the tournament that ends in a tie-break at 12-12.

Preferring not to participate in the Rogers Cup to rest, Novak Djokovic makes his comeback on hard court at the Masters 1000 in Cincinnati where he is the title holder. After three convincing wins in two sets against Sam Querrey (7-5, 6-1), Pablo Carreño Busta (6-3, 6-4) and Lucas Pouille (7-6, 6-1), he lost in the semifinals against the young Russian Daniil Medvedev after winning the first set (3-6, 6-3, 6-3)

He begins the defense of his title at the US Open by beating in the first three rounds, in 3 sets, the Spaniard Roberto Carballés Baena (6-4, 6-1, 6-4), the Argentine Juan Ignacio Londero (6-4, 7-6[3] , 6-1) and the American Denis Kudla (6-3, 6-4, 6-2) to find Stanislas Wawrinka in the round of 16, whom he had not faced since the final of the US Open 2016. It should be noted that the Serb has been suffering from a shoulder injury since the Masters 1000 in Cincinnati, which caused him to consider withdrawing during the second round match. But he said in a press conference after the third round that he was "almost pain free". However, he was forced to retire in the third set (6-4, 7-5, 2-1 ab.) after his injury reappeared. It was the first time since 2006 that he did not reach at least the semi-finals at Flushing Meadows.

For the first time in his career, he decided to travel to Tokyo for the Asian tour in preparation for the 2020 Olympics. He won the tournament without dropping a set, defeating Australia's Alexei Popyrin (6-4, 6-2), Japan's Go Soeda (6-3, 7-5), France's Lucas Pouille (6-1, 6-2), Belgium's David Goffin (6-3, 6-4) and finally Australia's John Millman (6-3, 6-2). At the Shanghai

Masters, after beating Canadian Denis Shapovalov (6-3, 6-3) and American John Isner (7-5, 6-3) in two sets, he lost to Greek Stéfanos Tsitsipás in three sets (3-6, 7-5, 6-3).

Weakened, Djokovic begins his indoor tour with the Paris-Bercy Masters and the certainty that he will lose his place as world number one to Rafael Nadal at the end of the tournament. In the first round, he defeated Frenchman Corentin Moutet in two sets (7-6,[2] , 6-4), then British Kyle Edmund (7-6,[7] , 6-1) and got his revenge against Greek Stéfanos Tsitsipás (6-1, 6-2). In the[e] semifinals, he defeated Bulgarian Grigor Dimitrov in two sets (7-6[5] , 6-4) in a high quality match to reach the 50e final of his career in a Masters 1000. He wins his 5e Masters de Paris-Bercy and his 34e Masters 1000 by disposing of the young Canadian Denis Shapovalov who is playing his first Masters 1000 final, in two sets (6-3, 6-4). With this title, he is one step closer to the record of Masters 1000 titles held by Rafael Nadal. This is his 77[e] ATP singles title, which allows him to join the top 5 most successful players in the history of tennis, equaling the American John McEnroe.

At the Masters he was eliminated in the group stage with a two-set victory (6-2, 6-1) over Italy's Matteo Berrettini and two defeats against Austria's Dominic Thiem in three sets (7-6[5] , 3-6, 6[5] -7) and Switzerland's Roger Federer in two sets (6-4, 6-3). This is the first time since 2011 that he did not pass the group stage, and at the same time he is guaranteed not to finish number one at the end of the year for the sixth time in his career in favor of Rafael Nadal.

2020: ATP Cup winner, 8e Australian Open title, record number of Masters 1000 titles (36) and number one for a record 6e year

Novak Djokovic enters the 2020 season with his sights set not only on the Grand Slam and Masters 1000 tournaments, but also the gold medal at the Tokyo Olympics. He returns to competition at the ATP Cup to prepare for his title defense in Melbourne. With Serbia, he won all his group matches against South Africa, beating Kevin Anderson (7-6^5 , 7-6^6), then against Gaël Monfils' France (6-3, 6-2) and finally against Chile, beating Cristian Garín (6-3, 6-3). He then defeated Denis Shapovalov's Canada (4-6, 6-1, 7-6^4), and in the semifinals, Russia by beating Daniil Medvedev (6-1, 5-7, 6-4). Finally against Spain, thanks to his victories in singles against the number 1 Rafael Nadal (6-2, 7-6^4) in their 55e confrontation and in doubles (as a team with Viktor Troicki) against the pair Feliciano Lopez-Pablo Carreño Busta (6-3, 6-4), he allows Serbia to win the first edition of the ATP Cup.

He began the defense of his title in Melbourne by defeating Germany's Jan-Lennard Struff in the first round in four sets (7-6^5 , 6-2, 2-6, 6-2) and then in the second and third rounds against Japan's Tatsuma Ito and Yoshihito Nishioka both in three sets (6-1, 6-4, 6-2) and (6-3, 6-2, 6-2). In the round of 16, he met the number 14 seed Diego Schwartzman of Argentina, whom he also beat without dropping a set (6-3, 6-4, 6-4) to reach his 46e Grand Slam quarter-final. He faced

Canadian Milos Raonic, whom he also defeated in three sets (6-4, 6-3, 7-6[1]) and thus reached the semifinals of a Grand Slam tournament for the 37e time against Swiss Roger Federer, whom he met again for the 50th time in his career. He won in three sets (7-6[1] , 6-4, 6-3) against a player who had been physically weak since the quarter-finals. This victory allows him to remain undefeated in the semi-finals of the Australian Open and to qualify for his 8e final in Melbourne where he is also undefeated. He won his 17e Grand Slam title against Austrian Dominic Thiem after a five-set match lasting nearly four hours (6-4, 4-6, 2-6, 6-3, 6-4). At the same time, he regained the number one ranking in the world at the expense of Rafael Nadal. By winning his eighth Australian Open, he becomes the third player in tennis history, along with Roger Federer and Rafael Nadal, to have at least eight Grand Slam titles in a single tournament. He also became the joint-record holder with Roger Federer of the number of Grand Slam titles won on hard courts (11), and one of only two players, along with Federer, to have won at least one Grand Slam title on five different courts, following the replacement of the Australian *Plexicushion* with the *Greenset*.

After a four-year absence in Dubai, he enters the tournament looking to win a fifth title. He began his tournament with quick wins in two sets against Tunisian Malek Jaziri (6-1, 6-2), German Philipp Kohlschreiber (6-3, 6-1) and Russian Karen Khachanov (6-2, 6-2). He then met Frenchman Gaël Monfils in the semifinals, who has had a remarkable start to the season. For their

17^e official meeting, he won in a breathtaking three-set match with three match points saved during the tie-break of the second set (2-6, 7-6^8 , 6-1). With this 17e victory without defeat against the Frenchman, he joins Roger Federer and Ivan Lendl who also managed to win 17 matches without defeat against other opponents. In the final, he faced the Greek number two seed, Stéfanos Tsitsipás, and won in two sets (6-3, 6-4) to win the 79e title of his career and secure his place as world number one. As the month of March begins, he remains undefeated with 18 wins and no losses.

In early March, the Covid-19 pandemic forced the ATP to suspend the season. Confined to Marbella in Spain for a while, Djokovic decided to return to Serbia in mid-May once the situation had improved and to organize an exhibition tournament in the Balkan countries, the Adria Tour. The organization does not apply protective measures (packed stadiums, no masks, close affection marks between players). The competition is stopped due to the contamination of several players, including Grigor Dimitrov, Borna Ćorić, Viktor Troicki, and Novak Djokovic himself. The latter later makes a public apology for the negligence.

Novak Djokovic resumes at the Cincinnati Masters where several players decided not to go to avoid contamination, including Rafael Nadal, Gaël Monfils and Stanislas Wawrinka. He won his first matches all in two sets against Lithuania's Ričardas Berankis (7-6^2 , 6-4), American Tennys Sandgren (6-2, 6-4) and Germany's Jan-Lennard Struff (6-3, 6-1) to reach the

68e semifinals of his Masters 1000 career. He won in an exciting three-hour match against Spain's Roberto Bautista-Agut in three sets (4-6, 6-4, 7-6^0), against whom he had lost three consecutive hard court matches. This victory allows him to play his 51e final in this category, equaling the record held by Rafael Nadal. He won the final against Canadian Milos Raonic in three sets (1-6, 6-3, 6-4) and once again became the joint-record holder of 35 Masters 1000 titles with Rafael Nadal. In addition, being the only player to have completed the Career Golden Masters, he becomes with this victory the only singles player to have won all tournaments in the Masters 1000 category at least twice.

The following week, he started the US Open as a big favorite. He won his first round match against Bosnian Damir Džumhur in three sets (6-1, 6-4, 6-1) and then "got rid" of British Kyle Edmund in four sets (6^5 -7, 6-3, 6-4, 6-2) and German Jan-Lennard Struff in three sets (6-3, 6-3, 6-1). On September 6, in the round of 16 against Spain's Pablo Carreño Busta, the Serbian was frustrated after being broken when minutes earlier he had three set points to win the first set. Unfortunately, after that, he was disqualified for hitting a ball he had left in his hand towards the back of the court without looking at it, which hit a line judge violently in the throat. This[e] is the 5th disqualification of a player in a Grand Slam since the beginning of the Open era. The defeat also ended a 26-match winning streak for the Serbian in 2020.

He starts the short season on clay (moved to the end of the summer) at the Masters of Rome, which includes the Spaniard Rafael Nadal back to competition after six months off. For his first match, he beat the Italian Salvatore Caruso and then his compatriot Filip Krajinović both in two sets (6-3, 6-2) and (7-6[7], 6-3). In the quarterfinals, he defeated German qualifier Dominik Köpfer in three sets (6-3, 4-6, 6-3) to advance to his 69[e] Masters 1000 semifinal where he defeated Norwegian Casper Ruud in two sets (7-5, 6-3). He becomes the first player to reach a 52[e] final in this category. He defeats Diego Schwartzman of Argentina in two sets (7-5, 6-3) to win his 5[e] title in Rome. On this occasion, he became the only record holder of titles in the Masters 1000 category (36) but also the oldest player to win a Masters 1000 on clay (33 years and 4 months).

He starts the French Open by beating the young Swedish Mikael Ymer in the first round in three sets (6-0, 6-2, 6-3). In the second round he defeated the Lithuanian Ričardas Berankis also in three sets (6-1, 6-2, 6-2) and won his 70[e] match at Roland Garros. He becomes the only player with Roger Federer to have at least seventy wins in all four Grand Slam tournaments. He easily qualifies for his 47[e] quarterfinals in Grand Slam, including a 14[e] at Roland Garros, record co-holder with Rafael Nadal, by beating successively the Colombian Daniel Elahi Galán and the Russian Karen Khachanov in three sets (6-0, 6-3, 6-2) and (6-4, 6-3, 6-3) He qualified for the 38[e] Grand Slam semifinals of his career, including the 10[e] Porte d'Auteuil, by beating Spain's Pablo Carreño Busta in four sets (4-6, 6-2, 6-3,

6-4) despite a bandaged neck. After his match, he admits to having felt discomfort during the preparation of the match. He also becomes only the third player (with Jimmy Connors and Roger Federer) in the Open Era to reach at least ten semifinals in at least two Grand Slams. He defeated Greece's Stéfanos Tsitsipás in five sets (6-3, 6-2, 5-7, 4-6, 6-1), after disposing of a match point in the third set, and reached his 27e Grand Slam final, including the 5e at Roland Garros. With this victory, he equals the record of Rafael Nadal and Roger Federer who have participated in at least five finals in the four Grand Slam tournaments. He faces Rafael Nadal for the ninth time in a Grand Slam final, equaling the record of Roger Federer and Rafael Nadal who have met in as many Grand Slam finals. He lost badly in three sets (0-6, 2-6, 5-7) to the Spaniard, who equaled Roger Federer's record of 20 Grand Slam titles.

With a view to securing a sixth record year as world number one at the end of the year, the Serb decides to play the ATP 500 in Vienna and to forego the Masters 1000 in Paris-Bercy, as the latter could not bring any points. He won his first match against his compatriot Filip Krajinović in two sets (7-6^6 , 6-3), then the second, against the Croatian Borna Ćorić also in two sets (7-6^{11} , 6-3), thus ensuring that he will finish as world number one in 2020, unless Rafael Nadal manages a clean sweep until the London Masters and the Serbian does not win any other match. In the quarter-finals, with little involvement, he suffered his heaviest defeat in his career since the 2005 Australian Open, against Italian Lorenzo Sonego in two sets (6-2, 6-1).

On November 6, with the non-participation of Rafael Nadal in the Sofia tournament, Novak Djokovic is guaranteed to finish the year at the top of the world rankings for a record sixth year, joining Pete Sampras at the top of the rankings with a lead over Roger Federer, Rafael Nadal and Jimmy Connors. In addition, at 33 years, 7 months and 9 days old as of December 31, 2020, he becomes the oldest player to finish a year atop the ATP rankings.

At the ATP Finals, which are being held in London for the last time, he is looking for a record sixth title to match Roger Federer. In the draw, he found himself in a pool with Daniil Medvedev (n° 4), Alexander Zverev (n° 6) and Diego Schwartzman (n° 8). In his first match, he defeated the Argentinean, who is a first-time participant, in two sets (6-3, 6-2). On the second day, he faced the Russian, a recent winner in Paris-Bercy. Unable to recognize and outplayed by the Russian player, he lost badly in two sets (6-3, 6-3). On the third day, he faced the German in a decisive match. He won in two sets (6-3, 7-6^4) and thus reached the last four, finishing second in his group behind Daniil Medvedev. In the semifinals, he faced the Austrian Dominic Thiem against whom he lost again in an epic match as in 2019 after saving four match points in the second set and after leading 4-0 in the decisive tie-break, he finally lost with the score of (5-7, 7-6^{10} , 6^5 -7).

After a beginning of season without any defeat, stopped by the Covid-19, Novak Djokovic realizes a second part of season more contrasted. His year of competition brought him four titles, including a Grand Slam and two Masters 1000. With a total of 41 wins and 5 losses, he finishes the year at the top of the ATP rankings with a lead of 2,180 points over his runner-up Rafael Nadal, bringing him closer to Roger Federer's record of 310 weeks at the top of the world ranking.

2021 : Petit Slam, 20e record Grand Slam title, record number of weeks at No. 1 and No. 1 for a 7e record year but disillusionment at the Olympics and US Open final

The start of the 2021 season has been delayed due to the Covid-19 pandemic and the strict health measures in place in Australia. Indeed, each player and their staff have to go through a fourteen day quarantine between January 17 and 31, which pushes the start of the Australian tour to February 1er .

For the second year in a row, Novak Djokovic decided to prepare for the Australian Open with Serbia by participating in the ATP Cup, of which it is the title holder. He first wins against Canada by beating Denis Shapovalov (7-5, 7-5) in singles and then, with his teammate Filip Krajinović in doubles, they beat the pair Milos Raonic and Denis Shapovalov (7-5, 7-6⁴). But his team was eliminated by Germany despite winning in three sets against Alexander Zverev (6³ -7, 6-2, 7-5) and losing in doubles with Nikola Čačić in three sets against the pair Alexander Zverev and Jan-Lennard Struff, (6⁴ -7, 7-5, [7-10]).

He won the title in Melbourne against Frenchman Jeremy Chardy in three sets (6-3, 6-1, 6-2). He then defeated American Frances Tiafoe, dropping a set (6-3, 6³ -7, 7-6² , 6-3). In the next round, while controlling his match against American Taylor Fritz and leading 2 sets to 0, he injured his abdominal muscles, which forced him to take several medical time-outs and anti-inflammatories and prevented him from moving properly on the court. He eventually won (7-6^1 , 6-4, 3-6, 4-6, 6-2) in a match that ended behind closed doors due to a lockdown in Victoria following several positive Covid-19 cases. In an interview, he said it was one of the best victories of his career, but he also thinks he has a tear that makes his participation in the round of 16 uncertain. In the next round, he defeated Canadian Milos Raonic in four sets (7-6^4 , 4-6, 6-1, 6-4) despite his injury, qualifying for his 48^e Grand Slam quarterfinals where he defeated German Alexander Zverev again in four sets (6^6 -7, 6-2, 6-4, 7-6^6). By qualifying for his 9^e semifinal at the Australian Open and the 39^e Grand Slam, he becomes the only player in the history of both men's and women's tennis to have reached the semifinals of all four Grand Slam tournaments at least nine times. He beat the surprise of the tournament, the Russian Aslan Karatsev from the qualifiers, in three sets (6-3, 6-4, 6-2) to qualify for his 9^e final in Melbourne and the 28^e in Grand Slam, equaling Rafael Nadal. In the final, he faced the number four seed, the Russian Daniil Medvedev, undefeated since the Paris-Bercy Masters (twenty wins in a row). The Serbian won his 9^e title in Melbourne and remains undefeated in the final by easily disposing of his opponent in three sets (7-5, 6-2, 6-2). With this victory, he becomes the only record holder of Grand Slam tournaments won on hard court (12) ahead of the Swiss Roger Federer (11). He also becomes the only one with Rafael Nadal to have won at least nine titles in a single

Grand Slam tournament, the Spaniard having won thirteen titles at Roland Garros since 2020.

On March 8, the Serbian began his 311e week as number one and became the record holder for weeks spent at the top of the ATP rankings, surpassing Switzerland's Roger Federer who had held the record since July 2012 (310 weeks).

He decided to skip the Miami Masters to rest. He made his return to prepare for the clay court season at the Monte Carlo Masters. After a quick victory over the revelation Jannik Sinner (6-4, 6-2), he was eliminated by the British Daniel Evans (6-4, 7-5), whom he faced for the first time in his career. The following week, he entered the Belgrade Open, a tournament owned by his family that was back on the calendar for the first time since 2012. He easily won his first two matches against South Korea's Kwon Soon-woo and his compatriot Miomir Kecmanović in two sets each time and by the same score (6-1, 6-3). In the semifinals, he played against the revelation of the year, the Russian Aslan Karatsev, to whom he lost after a match of more than three hours, in three sets (5-7, 6-4, 4-6).

After being forced to withdraw from the Madrid tournament, he returned to competition at the Rome Masters. In his first match, he defeated American Taylor Fritz in two sets (6-3, 7-6[5]), then Spanish Alejandro Davidovich Fokina in two sets (6-2, 6-1). In the quarter-finals, he faced the 5e world player, the Greek Stéfanos Tsitsipás. The match was interrupted on Friday due to weather conditions, with a score in favor of the Greek (4-6, 1-2), however, the next day he managed to reverse the course of the match and won in three sets (4-6, 7-5, 7-5) and 3 hours and 15 minutes of play. The same day, in his 70e Masters 1000 semifinal, he defeated Italian Lorenzo Sonego in three sets (6-3, 6^5-7, 6-2) and 2 hours and 44 minutes of play to reach the 53^e final in this category. He lost in three sets (5-7, 6-1, 3-6) against his great rival Rafael Nadal. This is the 9^e time that the two players meet in Rome, which is a record for the number of times the same two players have faced each other in a tournament. This 36^e victory in Masters 1000 allows the Spaniard to join the Serbian as the most successful player in this category.

After the French Open was moved up a week and the Belgrade tournament was added, he decided to play in the Serbian tournament, which is unusual for him in a week of a Grand Slam tournament. He won his first match against the German Mats Moraing in two sets (6-2, 7-6^5) and then against the Argentine Federico Coria in two sets (6-1, 6-0). This is the 952^e of the Serbian on the ATP circuit, which allows him to overtake the Argentine Guillermo Vilas and join the top 5 of the players who have won the most matches in his career. In the semifinals, he defeated Slovak qualifier Andrej Martin in three sets (6-1, 4-6, 6-0) and qualified for the 119^e final of his career against another Slovak, Alex Molčan. He won the final in two sets (6-4, 6-3) and won the 83^e title of his career, including the 16^e on clay, making him one of the top 10 most successful players on clay since the beginning of the Open Era.

Seeded number one at the French Open, he faced American Tennys Sandgren in the first round, beating him in three sets (6-2, 6-4, 6-2). In the second and third rounds, he defeated Uruguayan Pablo Cuevas (6-3, 6-2, 6-4) and Lithuanian Ričardas Berankis (6-1, 6-4, 6-1) in three sets each. Qualified for the round of 16, he became the first player to qualify in the second week at Roland Garros in twelve successive editions. He faced the young and promising Italian Lorenzo Musetti, whom he defeated in more than three hours of play after being down two sets to zero and finally winning by a dropout in the fifth set (6^7 -7, 6^2 -7, 6-1, 6-0, 4-0 ab.). He reached the 49[e] quarterfinals of his Grand Slam career, including the 15[e] at Roland Garros, a record he shares with Rafael Nadal. He is also the first player to reach the quarterfinals of the French Open 12 times in a row. He faced the number 9 seed, Matteo Berrettini of Italy, whom he beat in four sets (6-3, 6-2, 6^5 -7, 7-5), qualifying for his 40[e] Grand Slam semifinal, the 11th[e] at the French Open. He will meet his rival Rafael Nadal for a 58[e] confrontation, on 9[e] in Paris, which is a record for confrontations between two players in the same tournament. After a match lasting 4 hours and 11 minutes, he managed to beat the Spaniard in four sets (3-6, 6-3, 7-6^4 , 6-2) for the second time at Roland Garros. The Spaniard had a record of 105 wins in 107 matches played in the tournament. Novak Djokovic beat him for the 30[e] time in his career and qualified for his 29e Grand Slam final, the 6e at Roland Garros. This is a new record for the Serbian who is now the only player in the Open Era to have reached at least the final six times in all four Grand Slam tournaments. He won his 2e Roland Garros, beating the Greek Stéfanos Tsitsipás, in an intense match of 4 hours and 11 minutes again, and 5 sets (6^6 -7, 2-6, 6-3, 6-2, 6-4) after being led two sets to zero, which had not happened in the final of Roland Garros since 2004. He is only the 6e player to come back from a two-set deficit in a Grand Slam final and the first to win a title after two matches with such a handicap in the same tournament. In addition, he becomes the first player in the Open Era to win all four Grand Slams at least twice and the third in tennis history after Roy Emerson and Rod Laver. He also became the first player in the Open Era to win the Australian Open and French Open in the same year. This is his 19^e Grand Slam title. He is now one away from the record held by Roger Federer and Rafael Nadal.

To prepare for Wimbledon, he decides to participate in the Majorca tournament in doubles with the Spaniard Carlos Gómez-Herrera. They reached the final but had to withdraw due to an injury to the Spaniard. He wins his first match against the young British Jack Draper, losing the first set (4-6, 6-1, 6-2, 6-2). He then went on to defeat South Africa's Kevin Anderson (6-3, 6-3, 6-3), American Denis Kudla (6-4, 6-3, 7-6^7) and Chile's Cristian Garín, the number 17 seed, without dropping a set (6-2, 6-4, 6-2). This is the 50^e quarterfinal of his Grand Slam career, including the 12^e at Wimbledon. He defeats the Hungarian Márton Fucsovics in 3 sets (6-3, 6-4, 6-4) to qualify for the 41^e semifinals of his career in Grand Slam, including the 10^e in London where he faces the Canadian Denis Shapovalov. He won the match in three sets (7-6^3 , 7-5, 7-5) and qualified for the 30^e final of his Grand Slam career, including the 7^e in Wimbledon. Thus he becomes the first player since Björn Borg in 1980 to reach the final of the third Grand Slam of the season after winning the first two. He is also the first and only player in the history of tennis to play a 9^e Grand Slam final after his 30th birthday. He won his 6^e title at Wimbledon by beating Italian Matteo Berrettini, seeded number 7, in 4 sets (6^4 -7, 6-4, 6-4, 6-3). This is the 20^e Grand Slam title of his career, allowing him to become co-record holder of titles with Roger Federer and Rafael Nadal. Also, he is the first player since Rod Laver in 1969 to have won the first three Grand Slam tournaments of the year and therefore still be in contention for the calendar Grand Slam. He is also now the only player with Roger Federer to have won at least 6 Grand Slam titles in two different tournaments. Furthermore, with a 3^e Petit Slam, he equals Roger Federer's record. He is only the 4^e player of the Open Era to do the Roland Garros - Wimbledon double in the same season.

On July 16, he confirmed his participation in the Olympic Games in order to win the only Major title he is missing. After his three Grand Slam titles, he is two wins away from the *Golden Slam*, if he can win the Olympic gold medal and then win the US Open (a feat that only Steffi Graf accomplished in 1988). He starts as the overwhelming favorite and takes advantage of a clear field, with the withdrawals of Rafael Nadal, Roger Federer and Dominic Thiem in particular. He began with

three easy wins, all in two sets, against Bolivian Hugo
Dellien (6-2, 6-2) in the first round, German Jan-
Lennard Struff (6-4, 6-3) in the second round and
Spanish Alejandro Davidovich Fokina (6-3, 6-1) in the
third round. In the quarter-finals, he defeated Japan's
Kei Nishikori (6-2, 6-0). His dream of achieving the
Golden Grand Slam was defeated by Alexander Zverev
in the semifinals, who eliminated him in three sets (6-1,
3-6, 1-6) on July 30. Djokovic lost the small final against
Pablo Carreño Busta (4-6, 7-6^3 , 3-6) and as in 2012
finished at the foot of the podium. In the aftermath, he
withdrew from the small final of the mixed doubles he
was to play with Nina Stojanović, a withdrawal
motivated by a left shoulder injury.

For the first time in his career, the Serb starts the US
Open without any preparation tournament in Canada
and Cincinnati to try for the calendar Grand Slam. He
won his first match against the young Danish qualifier
Holger Rune in four sets (6-1, 6^5 -7, 6-2, 6-1). In the
second round, he defeated Tallon Griekspoor from the
Netherlands in 3 sets (6-2, 6-3, 6-2). He qualifies for the
51^e quarterfinals of his career in Grand Slam, including
the 12^e at the US Open by beating successively in 4
sets, the Japanese Kei Nishikori (6^4 -7, 6-3, 6-3, 6-2)
and the American Jenson Brooksby (1-6, 6-3, 6-2, 6-2).
He faced the Italian Matteo Berrettini, two months after
their final at Wimbledon, whom he beat in four sets (5-7,
6-2, 6-2, 6-3) to qualify for the 42^e semifinals of his
career in Grand Slam, including the 12^e at the US
Open. With this victory, he became the player with the
most wins over top 10 players in his career (224 wins to

101 losses). He took his revenge from the Olympic Games and defeated Alexander Zverev of Germany in five sets (4-6, 6-2, 6-4, 4-6, 6-2) to reach a 9e final at the US Open, a unique record in the Open Era, but also for the 31e final in the Grand Slam equaling the record of Roger Federer. In the final, he faced the Russian Daniil Medvedev, whom he had already beaten in the final of the Australian Open earlier this year. Very quickly, the match turns to the advantage of the number two seed who relies on an efficient service game while the Serb does not seem to be at his level and makes many mistakes. In two hours, the match was won by the Russian in three sets (4-6, 4-6, 4-6) and the dream of achieving the calendar Grand Slam came to an end for Djokovic, who was moved by the cheers of the crowd, who were all for him.

On September 29, he announced on social networks that he will not take part in the Masters of Indian Wells, leaving doubt about his participation in the end of year tournaments.

On October 18, he confirmed that he will participate in the Paris-Bercy Masters, the Masters and the Davis Cup.

At the Paris-Bercy Masters, he won his first match since the US Open final against Hungary's Márton Fucsovics in three sets (6-2, 4-6, 6-3) and then took advantage of Gaël Monfils' withdrawal to qualify for his 87e quarter-final in a Masters 1000 tournament, beating American Taylor Fritz in two sets (6-4, 6-3) to reach his 71e semifinal. He defeated Hubert Hurkacz of Poland in 3 sets (3-6, 6-0, 7-6^5) to reach a record 54^e final in this category. This victory guarantees him to finish the season at the top of the world rankings for the seventh time, one more time than the previous record holder Pete Sampras. In the final, Novak Djokovic defeated defending champion Daniil Medvedev of Russia in three sets (4-6, 6-3, 6-3) and won the Paris-Bercy Masters 1000 for the sixth time. This is the 86^e title of his career and the 37^e Masters 1000. He is also only the 3^e player to successfully win the French Open and Paris-Bercy in the same season after Ilie Năstase in 1973 and Andre Agassi in 1999.

At the ATP Finals, which are being held in Turin for the first time, he is looking for a record sixth title to equal Roger Federer. In the draw, he found himself in the pool of Stéfanos Tsitsipás (n° 4), Andrey Rublev (n° 5) and Casper Ruud (n° 8). For his first match, he beat the Norwegian, whose participation is his first, in two sets (7-6^4 , 6-2). On the second day, he played the Russian for the first time and beat him easily in two sets (6-3, 6-2). On the third day, following the withdrawal of the Greek Stéfanos Tsitsipás, he is opposed to the British substitute Cameron Norrie. He won in 2 sets (6-2, 6-1) and reached the last four finishing first in his group ahead of Casper Ruud. In the semifinals, he faced the German Alexander Zverev against whom he lost in 3 sets (6^4 -7, 6-4, 3-6).

Before ending a historic season, he decided to take part with Serbia in the 2020-2021 Davis Cup edition. The group stage is held in Innsbruck, Austria, with Austria and Germany as opponents. The Serbian team defeats Austria 3-0 with Djokovic winning the singles match against Dennis Novak in 2 sets (6-3, 6-2). They then lost to Germany 2-1 despite Novak winning in singles against Jan-Lennard Struff in 2 sets (6-2, 6-4) but losing in doubles with teammate Nikola Čačić against the pair Kevin Krawietz - Tim Pütz in 3 sets (6^5 -7, 6-3, 6^5 -7). Being one of the two best teams to finish 2^e , Serbia is qualified for the quarterfinals where they face Kazakhstan. The team qualifies for the semi-finals after Novak Djokovic won his singles match against Alexander Bublik in 2 sets (6-3, 6-4) and then in doubles with Čačić against the pair Andrey Golubev - Aleksandr Nedovyesov in 3 sets (6-2, 2-6, 6-3). In the semifinals, they were eliminated against Croatia despite Djokovic winning against Marin Čilić in 2 sets (6-4, 6-2) but losing to the best doubles team in the world Nikola Mektić - Mate Pavić in 2 sets with Filip Krajinović (7-5, 6-1).

2022: Difficult start to the season, expelled from Australia for non-vaccination, banned from entering the USA, return and failure in Monte-Carlo

Novak Djokovic is scheduled to start his 2022 season with the Australian Open. After several months of media speculation, with his vaccination status unknown, Djokovic confirmed his participation in the tournament on January 4, due to a medical exemption from the mandatory vaccination that applies in the state of Victoria. The decision to give Djokovic a medical exemption by the organizers was criticized by Prime Minister Scott Morrison, who stated that the player must provide proof of his medical exemption or take "the first plane home". On January 5, Djokovic's visa was cancelled and deportation proceedings forced him to leave the country on January 6, jeopardizing his participation in the tournament. However, he appealed and was detained in a hotel in Melbourne for people who arrived in Australia illegally. In addition, it is revealed that the exemption granted to Djokovic by the Australian tennis authorities is, according to his lawyers, due to the fact that he contracted Covid-19: he would have tested positive on December 16, 2021. The review of his appeal is studied on January 10 by the Australian authorities, to determine whether he must leave the territory or not. A judge reinstated his visa and ordered Djokovic's release. However, Immigration Minister Alex Hawke cancelled the player's visa again on January 14 "on the grounds of health, public order and that it was in the public interest to do so". The Serbian's lawyers filed an appeal. On 15 January, he was returned to administrative detention. On January 16, the federal court rejected Novak Djokovic's appeal against his deportation, with no possibility of appeal. He left the Australian territory the same day. Djokovic will not play in the 2022 Australian Open and will be replaced by the Italian *lucky loser* Salvatore Caruso . The Australian Tennis Federation and the State of Victoria misled players, including Djokovic and Renata Voráčová, into believing that a simple past infection with the virus is sufficient to participate in the tournament, while vaccination is required to enter Australia.

The case earned Djokovic the nickname "Novax Djocovid" on social networks and in some media . For the French daily *Le Parisien*, "Whatever the outcome, the "Novax Djocovid" affair will profoundly mark the image of the most controversial player in the world of tennis. In *Libération*, the press cartoonist Coco published on January 10, 2022 a cartoon titled "Novax" showing the player handling a tennis ball in the shape of a virus, while the crocodile embroidered on his shirt comments "Djocovid for the intimates". *Le Figaro*, for its part, speaks of "Novak Gate".

On February 15, he gave an exclusive interview to the BBC in which he explained that he did not want to be vaccinated for the time being and that he was "prepared to miss the French Open and Wimbledon rather than be vaccinated.

He resumes competition at the Dubai tournament where he wins against the Italian Lorenzo Musetti and the Russian Karen Khachanov in 2 sets (6-3, 6-3) and (6-3, 7-6^2). He lost in the quarterfinals to Czech Jiří Veselý in 2 sets (3-6, 6^4 -7).

Banned from entering the USA for non-vaccination, he cannot play the Masters 1000 in Indian Wells and Miami.

For the clay court season, he is allowed to play in Monte Carlo, where he loses in the second round against the future finalist of this edition, the Spaniard Alejandro Davidovich Fokina in 3 sets (3-6, 7-6^5 , 1-6) and 2 hours 55 minutes of play. The following week, he participated in his tournament in Belgrade, where he defeated his compatriot Laslo Djere in the second round in three sets (2-6, 7-6^6 , 7-6^4) and three hours and 21 minutes of play. He then won in 3 sets against Serbian Miomir Kecmanović (4-6, 6-3, 6-3) and Russian Karen Khachanov (4-6, 6-1, 6-2) to reach the 124^e final of his career. He lost it against the number 2 seed Andrey Rublev in 3 sets (2-6, 7-6^4 , 0-6) after notably indicating that he had lost all his energy after winning the second set and blamed the illness he has been carrying for more than two weeks.

He participates in the Madrid tournament for the first time since 2019, where he faces for his debut the Frenchman Gael Monfils, whom he beats in 2 sets (6-3, 6-2). With this 18^e victory without defeat against the Frenchman, he becomes the first tennis player to beat an opponent so many times without ever having conceded a single defeat. With the withdrawal of British Andy Murray, he directly qualifies for the 88[e] quarterfinals in Masters 1000 in which he beats Polish Hubert Hurkacz in two sets (6-3, 6-4) and reaches his 72[e] semifinal. He lost to Spain's Carlos Alcaraz in a three-set match lasting 3 hours and 35 minutes (7-6[5], 5-7, 6[5] -7).

At the Rome Masters, he successively defeated Russian Aslan Karatsev (6-3, 6-2), then Swiss Stanislas Wawrinka (6-2, 6-2), before meeting Canadian Felix Auger-Aliassime whom he met and defeated for the first time in two sets (7-5, 7-6[1]), thus qualifying for his 73[e] Masters 1000 semifinal. He reached his 55[e] Masters 1000 final with a two-set victory over Casper Ruud of Norway (6-4, 6-3). This is his 1000[e] career win on the ATP circuit, becoming the fifth player to reach this total after Jimmy Connors (1274), Roger Federer (1251, active), Ivan Lendl (1068) and Rafael Nadal (1051, active). In the final, he defeated Greece's Stéfanos Tsitsipás in two sets (6-0, 7-6[5]) to win his 6e title in Rome. On this occasion, he wins his 38e Masters 1000, which allows him to take a two-unit lead over Rafael Nadal in the ranking of the number of titles in Masters 1000 but also to become the oldest player to win a Masters 1000 on clay (34 years, 11 months and 23 days).

He enters the 2022 French Open as the number one seed to defend his title. In the first round he met the Japanese Yoshihito Nishioka, whom he beat in three sets (6-3, 6-1, 6-0). In the second round he met the Slovak Alex Molčan, now coached by Marián Vajda, whom he also beat in three sets (6-2, 6-3, 7-6). He then easily defeated the Slovenian Aljaž Bedene (6-3, 6-3, 6-2) and the Argentine Diego Schwartzman (6-1, 6-3, 6-3) and thus qualified for his 16[e] quarter-finals at the Paris Grand Slam, where he met Rafael Nadal for a 59[e] duel, which he lost in four sets (2-6, 6-4, 2-6, 6[4] -7)

Characteristics of his game

Novak Djokovic is considered one of the most complete players on the circuit. His attack-defense balance is considered the best on the circuit, as he is so good in both areas. He is characterized by an "offensive counter style" based on his exceptional physicality. His coverage of the field is indeed considered excellent, he moves very quickly, changes direction abruptly and knows how to manage his physical condition very well. Very difficult to overrun, he excels in the distribution of the game by printing an infernal rhythm to the exchange which becomes difficult to bear for his opponent.

His strong point is his return of serve, which is considered the most formidable on the circuit. His very good technique, anticipation and reflexes allow him to counter the opponent's first balls and to regularly take the upper hand on the second ones. In addition, he doesn't take many aces or winning serves. He also has one of the best backhands in the world. While his forehand is solid, his backhand is even more so, like Lleyton Hewitt and David Nalbandian. Especially on the flat, he is able to move the ball at a very high pace and hit any area of the court. Regardless of his position, he is always in a good position to make that shot. He has also learned how to slice it to get to the net on grass and his backhand bunt, which is mostly hidden, is particularly fearsome. On the forehand side, he can also be very dangerous, whether it's down the line or on the diagonals, lifted or flat, but it's when he goes for the short crosscourt that his forehand is really the most powerful.

His main weaknesses are, as with most players today, in the pure attacking game. If the Serb is able to volley well when conditions are favorable, he cannot afford to go up against the clock or in difficult circumstances, unlike a specialist like Roger Federer. However, Djokovic is able to go to the net regularly, like in the 2012 US Open final against Andy Murray (39 points won out of 56 approaches to the net). During the 2013 Australian Open final, which he won against Murray, he posted exceptional statistics at the net, winning 35 out of 41 attempts. Starting with the 2013 US Open, he hired Wojtek Fibak as an advisor, especially to improve his volleying. The effects are noticeable, with once again an excellent success rate at the net against Juan Martín del Potro when they met in the final of the

Shanghai Masters and in the pool match of the London Masters. Although relatively good, the Serbian's serve, even after improving at the height of his dominance in 2010, is not one of his strong points, despite a first ball that can slam aces on important points and a second ball of great quality. Novak Djokovic is often compared to Lleyton Hewitt, with less skill at the net, but with a more powerful game from the baseline. One of Djokovic's strengths is his versatility in adapting to any surface.

Equipment and sponsors

Novak Djokovic uses the *Head Youtek IG Speed MP 315* racquet. Since his arrival on the professional circuit, Djokovic has worn Adidas clothing and shoes. At the end of 2009, Djokovic signed a ten-year contract with Italian tennis equipment manufacturer Sergio Tacchini. However, he continues to wear Adidas shoes, and more precisely since 2011, the Red & Blue Adidas Barricade 6.0, with the colors of the Serbian flag where he continues to wear them until mid 2012 to then change them for Adidas Barricade 7.0 with colors chosen by Novak Djokovic himself: the Black/Grey, the White/Grey or the White/Blue/Red which are the colors of the Serbian flag. On May 23, 2012, Novak Djokovic signed a five-year contract with the Japanese equipment manufacturer Uniqlo. Sergio Tacchini, which was his equipment supplier for more than two years, ended the contract that bound him to Djokovic. The reason given by the brand is the cost became too important that the tennis player represents following his various sporting successes; the company could no longer supply the distribution network with equipment that the Serbian wore. In early 2014, Djokovic announced two partnerships: one with Peugeot, a brand for which he became an international ambassador for the next three years, and the other with Seiko, with whom he also signed a three-year contract. On the occasion of the 2017 French Open, the Serb signs with the equipment manufacturer Lacoste for a period of five years.

Personality

He is known to have a great sense of humor: we have seen a good number of reports where he "entertains the gallery", even before some very big matches (notably in the semi-finals of the US Open in 2007). He has a certain talent for imitating most of the players on the circuit, in particular Maria Sharapova, Rafael Nadal, Andy Roddick or even Roger Federer whom he imitated in the locker room during a tournament.

He is a fan of Red Star Belgrade in Serbia, AC Milan in Italy, Manchester United in England, AS Monaco in France, Real Madrid in Spain and Benfica in Portugal.

In 2010, he made an appearance in the clip of Martin Solveig and Dragonette *Hello*.

On November 30, 2011, he was selected to make a brief appearance in the film *Expendables 2: Special Unit* by Simon West, which was released in August 2012, alongside Sylvester Stallone, Arnold Schwarzenegger, Chuck Norris, Bruce Willis, Jet Li and many others. Finally, the scene is cut in the editing.

Lifestyle

Novak Djokovic is said to be allergic to gluten; he revealed this information in April 2011 when he started a gluten-free diet seven months ago. Since then, he said he feels better on the court. He also declared in May 2016 to have a pesco-vegetarian or even vegan diet.

In April 2016, together with his wife, shortly before the start of the Monte Carlo Masters, they opened a vegan restaurant in the same city called *Eqvita*. On the occasion of the opening, many players of the ATP circuit come there to taste something. In 2020, he declared that his plant-based diet was also based on altruism towards animals and environmental concerns. In 2021, his wife said that she did not influence him and that Novak Djokovic was the first to go vegan.

In January 2022, he triggered a controversy by refusing, in the context of the COVID-19 pandemic, to communicate his vaccination status, while the vaccine is mandatory to travel to Melbourne to play in the Australian Open. He was refused entry and his registration for the tournament was suspended. According to the sports sociologist Jean-Baptiste Guégan, the player is thus "the face of the antivax, because it is imagined that he is not vaccinated.

Positions taken in the world of tennis

Novak Djokovic declared himself in 2016 in favor of a new redistribution of tournament winnings. He believes that men should earn more than women for the same tournament. As such, he states that "statistics show that men's tennis attracts more people. In my opinion, this is one of the reasons why we need to touch more [...] As long as there is data on who attracts the most spectators, who sells the most tickets, he should be fairly rewarded."

At the beginning of 2018, on the sidelines of the Australian Open, he wants for the players an increase in retributions. He believes that, given the increase in the endowments of tournaments, the rate reserved for players must increase because would become too low. According to the press, he advocates the creation of a players' union to be more present in negotiations with the ATP, but Novak Djokovic has denied these allegations. If this project exists, it is still not completed. Nevertheless, the idea has been taken up by Vasek Pospisil.

In 2019, on the sidelines of the Indian Wells Masters, the departure of ATP President Chris Kermode is announced following a vote by the Board of Directors. Novak Djokovic, who is a member of the board as president of the players is designated by the press and players as the person responsible for this decision. Defending an increase in players' income and publicly denouncing Chris Kermode's attitude of siding with tournament organizers who were not in favor of this measure, Novak Djokovic made sure that the re-election vote of the ATP president was against him. Shortly afterwards, Rafael Nadal criticized this electoral failure publicly stating that "it is likely that those who represent us on the players' council have not done their job well. I was disappointed that they did not bother to call me to inform me. " . Novak Djokovic, through this incident, is now seen as a maneuverer. Jean-François Caujolle, then director of the Open 13, said of Djokovic "that he seeks power [...] that he has a perspective for the future. [...] He wants to make his mark on the game and impose his vision on the organization. This crisis led to the reinstatement of Roger Federer and Rafael Nadal to the players' council a few months after the incident.

Due to major fires in early 2020 in Australia, Novak Djokovic is considering a postponement of the Australian Open. He says "if the conditions affect the health of the players, yes we have to think about it. But it's probably the very last option to consider [...] because there's a schedule to keep and a lot of things are at stake. But health is a concern for me and everyone else."

During the 2020 season heavily affected by the Covid-19 pandemic, Novak Djokovic proposes, in an open letter, the creation of a support fund, financed by the 100 best players in singles and the 20 best in doubles, for professional players ranked between 250^e and 700^e places. This initiative, which has been supported by

Roger Federer and Rafael Nadal, sets a sliding scale according to the ranking of the players and would raise more than one million euros. This proposal is part of a more global fundraising effort, as the ATP and the Grand Slam tournaments are also being asked for funding.

On August 29, 2020, he decided to resign as president of the Players Council along with fellow players John Isner and Vasek Pospisil to create a new players' association, the *Professional Tennis Players Association*.

Professional Tennis Players Association

At his initiative and those of Canadian Vasek Pospisil and American John Isner, August 29, 2020 sees the creation of an association of players, the *Professional Tennis Players Association*, feared by the ATP since its inception. Roger Federer and Rafael Nadal have publicly stated that they do not support this project.

Personal activities

In 2008, Novak Djokovic bought the rights to the Amersfoort Open in the Netherlands and moved it to Belgrade.

Adria Tour case

While the ATP circuit should not resume before the end of July because of the COVID-19 crisis, the Serbian decided to organize the Adria Tour, an event spread over several weeks through the Balkan countries, less affected than Western Europe by the epidemic, and bringing together several tennis stars, in a two-day round-robin format before a final between the best of each group. The first stage, played in Belgrade with an audience, was won by Dominic Thiem, with Novak Djokovic failing to top his group after a loss to Filip Krajinović.

The following weekend (June 20-21), the Adria Tour moved to Zadar and from the first match, the alarm was raised. In his face-off with Borna Ćorić, the Bulgarian Grigor Dimitrov seems weakened and gives up. Upon his return to Monaco, he tested positive for COVID-19 and the final of the stage, which was supposed to oppose the Russian Andrey Rublev to Novak Djokovic, is canceled. From there, Novak Djokovic's decision to organize this event without any barrier and with a public, as well as the extras of the tournament (nightclub outings, a basketball match, a "Kids Day", etc.) are strongly reproached. In the following days, it was the turn of Borna Ćorić and Viktor Troicki to test positive, before the world number one was also confirmed positive on Tuesday, June 23. While his image has already been damaged, no sanctions are expected against the Serbian, but this event casts doubt on the resumption of the tour, scheduled for August. Shortly after the announcement, various players of the circuit, like Nick Kyrgios and Andy Murray, reacted by criticizing the organization of this competition and reminding that precautions should be taken.

During the lock-in, Novak Djokovic had already taken several controversial positions. He refuses the idea of a mandatory vaccination against the coronavirus, takes a stand against the hygienic measures proposed for the US Open, disseminates videos of his recovery (considered by some as too early) on the courts in Spain and makes on his Instagram live the promotion of pseudoscientific products and theories[11] .

Humanitarian actions

The Novak Fund, now the Novak Djokovic Foundation

Novak Djokovic is committed to his country, and not only in a sporting way. In November 2007, Novak Djokovic created a charity organization, the *Novak Fund*, which became the *Novak Djokovic Foundation* in February 2012. The purpose of this foundation is to help Serbia and the Serbian people to face some difficulties because as a child, Novak Djokovic had to flee with his family the 80 days of bombing of Belgrade by the NATO forces. He still considers this period to be the hardest of his life. Today, the foundation focuses primarily on efforts to educate disadvantaged children. In May 2014, he donated all of his winnings from his victory at the Rome Masters to all of the disaster victims in his country who were victims of unprecedented flooding.

In 2012, Novak Djokovic received the Arthur-Ashe Award for his humanitarian commitment as an ambassador for UNICEF, but also for the importance of his association, the Novak Djokovic Foundation.

In 2017, he announced the opening of a free restaurant in Serbia for the homeless and needy. In the announcement, he states "Money is not a problem for me. I have earned enough to feed all of Serbia. I think they deserve it after the support I received from them."

In January 2020, he made a donation to support the victims of the forest fires in Australia.

In March 2020, he donated one million euros to Serbia to help it fight the Covid-19 pandemic and provide medical equipment in hospitals. He makes another donation for a hospital in Bergamo, one of the hardest hit cities in Italy.

International activities

Novak Djokovic is a member of the "Champions for Peace" club, a group of high-level athletes created by Peace and Sport, an international organization based in Monaco and working to build sustainable peace through sport.

In July 2012, he was present at the UN headquarters for the establishment of April 6 as the International Day of Sport for Development and Peace. He was one of the seven Peace and Sport Champions for Peace who participated in a symbolic march organized by the Principality of Monaco to mark the 25^e anniversary of the International Convention on the Rights of the Child in 2015.

In 2012, he was awarded the Order of the Star of Karageorge, Serbia's highest honor, as well as the Vermeil Medal of Monaco for Physical Education and Sports, presented personally by Prince Albert II.In the same year, Prince William of Cambridge presented him with an award for his humanitarian commitment.

Relationship with Serbia

In October 2018, Novak Djokovic's father, Srdjan, revealed that in 2006 he was contacted by representatives of the British Embassy as well as representatives of their Tennis Federation who wanted to see Novak play for the British nation in Davis Cup with Andy Murray. For this, the British offered a lot of money and a better training situation. Novak Djokovic replied that "there is not a single force that could change this situation, we are Serbs and we will remain so until the end of our lives. But his love for his country does not close him in rancor. He said on January 3, 2019 for *Blic*: "The war did not bring anything to the countries of Yugoslavia, today I look at Croatia, Bosnia as brotherly countries. Many thanks to Luka Modrić, during the world cup I was always behind Croatia." He says that he likes to spend his vacations in Croatia with his family, saying that the Croatian coasts are the most beautiful in the world, that Croatians are friendly and because the Serbian and Croatian languages are close and there is a common culture between Serbia and Croatia.

Despite the support and money he brings[How ?] to Serbia, Novak Djokovic is nevertheless resident in Monaco since 2007, the year of his first appearance in the world top 10, which he justifies by the quality of sports facilities and safety on the rock.[réf. necessary]

Links with the Serbian Orthodox Church

On April 28, 2011, he is decorated by the Serbian Orthodox Church with the medal of St. Sava of the first order: he often makes significant donations for the renovation of the monasteries of Gracanica, Holy Exchanges and especially for the monastery of Hilandar. He declares on this occasion that it is for him "the most important title of his life, because before being a sportsman, he is an Orthodox Christian". On the same day, the Serbian Minister of Foreign Affairs Vuk Jeremić issued all Serbian tennis players a diplomatic passport, to facilitate their travel abroad.

In 2019, he is participating in the safeguarding of a Serbian chapel located in Nice.

Investment

In June 2020, he became a co-founder of QuantBioRes, a Danish biotech company researching a treatment for Covid-19.

Awards

Novak Djokovic has received numerous awards during his career, both from official (ATP) and unofficial (media, foundations) bodies, for both his sporting achievements and his personality (fair play, availability to the media).

Other books by United Library

https://campsite.bio/unitedlibrary